BANKING CORRUPT PRACTICES

LOOTERS AND PROTECTORS
(INDIAN EDITION)

ARKO A

PARTRIDGE

To order additional copies of this book, contact
Toll Free +65 3165 7531 (Singapore)
Toll Free +60 3 3099 4412 (Malaysia)
orders.singapore@partridgepublishing.com

www.partridgepublishing.com/singapore

CONTENTS

FOREWORD

In every activity, a decision can go wrong because of mistakes. Genuine mistakes are part of life and learning. However, decisions structured in such a way that a business fails as planned and the perpetrator of the decision-making process gets away, while institutions and people down the chain of command suffer at the hands of these structured acts, need to be looked at with greater scrutiny. The contents of this study, therefore, relate to corrupt practices, by Indians in connivance with certain people helping these perpetrators in India and overseas, that I have seen during my banking and entrepreneurial career.

In my life, the Gita's two quotes have played a very important role since 1988. These are:

1. Do your duty; reward is not thy concern
2. Whatever happened, happened for the good; whatever is happening is happening for the good; whatever will happen will happen for the good

Normally, people ask some luminary from the subject field to write the foreword. However, in the mysterious world of corruption or corrupt practices in the banking and financial industry involving Indians across the world, finding the right person in these times is difficult, and it is doubtful who is above board. Our country, for the first time, is headed by an upright prime minister, but seeing the corruption index of our country, we have something to think about. One cannot find out who is pretending to be honest. The question mark on their conduct is clearly visible. The best ideologies have also failed present-day India. Many times, those who pretend to stand for the truth are hypocrites and have not stood up for their advocacy when it mattered. People act not in the interest of humanity or their country but only for their own glory. The corrupt are becoming bolder day by day.

Given the situation, I have felt that I should write these lines and take responsibility for what I am penning here. The contents are factual and devoid of any hyperbole. This study covers wrong international trading practices and methodologies adopted by its practitioners. I had been firm in dealing with wrong practices up at the appropriate level within my bank, but efforts were not appreciated by the system. I had brought to light a few events during the course of my job to give evidence to reality (exhibit at the end). Now

I have reached the age and stage where I can afford to take on the real fight and have nothing to lose. My motivation comes from circumstances that most of us are not able to withstand. At the far end of life, it is better to reach the last mile with some factual truth.

I take this as the last challenge of my life. The write-up will be a little dull as it traverses through my almost four-decade journey in banking-related activities. A few pages are devoted to memories in the bank while the rest deal with real events. I am sure it will alert the financial field, particularly my banking colleagues who are engaged in handling trade-related appraisal and documentation at their respective banks. The reality is brought in front, and everyone can review with better application. A lot of people know but keep silent, particularly the promoters/CA/CFOs, including our controlling entities. This study leverages my experience of almost forty years and a detailed analysis over the last few years to get to this point of factual and sickening things happening to the banking and insurance sector which bleeds due to the greed of people running the show. Had it not been for the pandemic, these contents would have come out in the open a little earlier.

I do not know why I did not involve my immediate family. However, I knew one thing – family members would get disturbed, but keeping them away from really tough situations always felt good; to stay focussed is the goal in mind. I have nothing more to lose now once my life's goal is achieved and mental peace derived from the actions taken.

I am not going to elaborate as most of the bankers working in credit/forex/international trade will be able to make out what is being brought out in the following pages. I have tried to make it in two parts – one from my journey within the bank, covering various periods, and another from outside the bank with deep insight into Indian promoted corporates working overseas and their operating methods. This is important as without knowing the background, the script needs to traverse the path from the beginning which helps motivate events. To this day, new things come to our knowledge, and some help will definitely come through my effort in arresting the menace of wrong practices globally. Maybe the bleeding will slow down and culprits will be brought to book.

One thing that is clear in the Indian context is that those who speak the truth are harassed like hell; as a result, only few people come forward, or people just bear the burden of carrying adverse situations and leave the rest to destiny. Let us see how things unfold for me once this study in the form of a book comes out to the world.

PREFACE

Having served the banking industry for over thirty-seven years, I always wondered why bankers at the lower level are the easiest targets of wrong practices/corruption or procedural lapses by investigating agencies, while the hugely corrupt functionaries in large number in government departments are not nabbed. My experience says that bankers will be found the least corrupt when you compare them with those in various arms of government departments, where you can always categorise them with their level of corrupt practices and how much running around one has to do to get things moving. To top it all, the major mischief point in banking is the top management in many Public Sector Undertaking (PSU) banks and the government-appointed directors. These people are rarely penalised, but down the chain of authority, people are penalised for trivial issues. The chairman and managing directors (MD and CEO now) run the show and take all the members (directors) on board to keep things moving. The shrewder the person at the top, the bigger the manipulations that will be noticed over a period.

Directions for various big financial decisions come from the top; very rarely do you see them accepting justifiable advice from the team members.

I will say with commitment that bankers have moles among them, as people working in credit-related matters are more prone or can succumb to the temptation of corruption, while most of the other functionaries are totally public/non-public faces with full integrity and devotion to work. Service delivery comes with motivation and commitment, which can be created through teamwork by the leader. Frauds with staff involvement do happen, which can be checked with technology and proper vigilance.

I had to cut short my career as I, along with my team, was made victim of the wrong action of superiors protecting the corrupt, and the government investigating arm made us victim of procedural lapses without doing a real investigation. This was more a motivated campaign from within the bank by jealous colleagues. This brought deep anguish as the real culprits were enjoying, while I would have bad, depressive thoughts as I failed my juniors.

With my banking background and experience in credit, forex, international trade, and finance, I started my second inning in Hong Kong as an adviser cum entrepreneur with assistance from known business clients of the bank to help them in arbitrage business as well as structured trade throughout Hong Kong. This gave me the idea to find a working relationship with them to see real action in international trade and structured trade finance.

The motivation in writing this book came mainly when I saw a huge deviation at the bank level and corporate level, while people below are being penalised or punished for carrying out instructions. Initially, I did not think it as normal practice; but once in Hong Kong and on the other side of banking, working with corporates as an independent entity, I came across events which were eye-openers for me. Slowly and gradually, new things started unfolding. I became accidentally involved and then thought of converting this accident as an opportunity to learn. I did send anonymous feedback to the regulators/agencies on few occasions in India (attached at the end) but no actions were taken.

In my second year of coming to Hong Kong, I started to work on delving deep into the Indian business communities' wrong practices and siphoning of banking funds to bleed the system. It was a time-consuming exercise as one had to be pally with people to get the complete picture., but ultimately, a lot of chains slowly came to my knowledge which otherwise would not have been possible. Actual case studies in this book would make things clear to people who work in international banking and credit areas.

The reason in mind was clear – find out why bankers get sucked into corporate frauds and find out their modus operandi at the international level as the Indian side's truth-finding process is too shady, and without much support. While working overseas, one is independent. I had seen many Indian clients running away with huge sums borrowed overseas and vanish or move back to India, leading to jurisdiction issues in legal remedies. Within six months, the real games being played started coming to my knowledge where joint action was being made by corporates, top management people, bureaucrats, politicians, consultants, et al.

In this book, I would be using real events where I got directly or indirectly involved in the bank and corporate side. The challenge was more internal as I had decided that I would gain knowledge of what they were doing. The real challenge was that the top corporate people would not like to share what their plans were. Extracting this information was a real issue, as I did not want to give them any inkling of my plans. I kept major secrets to myself; otherwise, things would not have made their way into this book. Corporates use bankers as their tools, and I have used these very people to understand their tools. I am sure the factual incidents in this book will make all relevant people take note of facts and take some positive steps in saving the hard-earned money of the common man from these canny people.

INTRODUCTION: ONE SIDE OF THE COIN – BANK'S SIDE MEMORY LANE

The script starts from India and continues overseas. This part takes me to the start of my career and needs a little summary. I started my banking career in December 1976 as a clerk typist after two short stints in Uttar Pradesh State Government Services Tribunal during an emergency period and the Intelligence Bureau (IB) of the government of India. I left the state government job after two months as I could not stomach the corruption in courts, with the aggrieved paying for a favourable verdict. It was at the lower level only. Two other colleagues also left. IB did not offer a career, though it gave insight into the workings of the Ministry of Home Affairs.

Opportunity in the bank came, with friends saying that there was future in the banking industry. Yes, my friends were right. Within seven years, I was an officer in a very good PSU bank. The seven lucky years saw me work as a typist in the controlling office with focus on audit follow-up, credit proposals, balance sheet, vigilance function, and then branch banking. The bank also gave me enough opportunity in sporting activities and study for career planning. I had no regrets and only gains through interaction with quality officers and books.

The journey as an officer commenced in December 1983 and straight into the credit department in a semi-urban centre where the bank also had a lead bank role. It was in Janardan Pujari's time, when loan under various government schemes was the order of the day – Self-employment for Educated Unemployed Youth, Self-employment Programme for Urban Poor, Differential Rate Interest scheme, Integrated Rural Development Programme (IRDP), SC/ST schemes. All these schemes were target-oriented where commitment cut had already been taken care of by various government departments. They would tell the prospective candidates that they had sanctioned and that the bank had to disburse. This was misguidance and getting rid of the problem at their end.

Once the ball was in the court of the bank, the heat is on the officer assigned to carry out pre-sanction inspections and recommend the loan for approval. The applications under all categories would number to a few hundred, with distances of ten to fifteen kilometres to be covered running in villages around the branch. Many times, you would be cornered by ruffians/political parties' grassroots workers who would threaten you to no end and try to corrupt you to recommend and let the disbursement happen. It was a tough time; colleagues came to the rescue in such situations on the road. Majority of the loans under this segment would go bad from day one as funds would be diverted, or the business would fail due to inexperience.

Similar situations continued when I was moved as manager to a rural branch, but at least people there made efforts to do some business, and failure would not come overnight. This was the difference I noticed between cities and rural areas. I went to bigger centres over the years, with my function remaining as part of the credit field. The real colours of some seniors were visible, and as you move up, you can see what is happening at the top. Bank employees were getting a bad name for the bad work done by a handful at the top, from branch head to bank head.

We are now used to hearing banking frauds of various kinds done by corporates. Central Bureau of Investigation, Chief Vigilance Commission, Enforcement Directorate, and all other regulatory authorities go after bankers and corporates. Both corporates & government arms have vested interest in cornering and painting a bad picture of junior employees at banks, but behind the scenes, games of different kinds are played. Nobody seems to get into the bottom of the real issues, and feet are dragged in such a way that the real problem is forgotten. Resultantly, bankers at the lower level get penalised, and loan money seldom comes back to the lending bank.

I always wondered about the games being played, particularly at the boardroom and among the corporates who are always hungry for money through all possible means. *Crooked* is the more appropriate word. In reality, major failures of the corporates are due to management's fault rather than real business failure. Once in the saddle, the greed to grow beyond their means takes over, and things start moving from one to ten directions. This leads to resources moving in all directions, and all pulls are taking the resources to a number of routes and ultimately losing track. At the end of the day, the bank is staring at an entire loss, while the promoter corporate is able to take his part, and the rest is left to the vultures to eat.

Having served a **PSU** bank in various capacities, including in overseas markets, I always wondered why the top management has to get involved in mobilising businesses, why the business coming to them is not passed on to the team responsible to carry out due diligence and then prepare the paper for discussion and, in principle, approval. The top management decides first after meeting with corporate top guns and then ask teams working down the line to prepare papers per their commands. This has led to serious problems in large-value loans and facilities where ground-level functionaries are always under pressure to perform based on the directions rather than having any knowledge of the business they are going to handle. Everything comes from the top, and promoters use this as a tool to commit procedural lapses. Company honchos can be interviewed initially at the branch level rather than the top executive/top management level, where no basics are attended. This makes the entire decision process distorted.

Having said that and having seen the bank's side and learned the lessons the hardest way, it was time to get into the shoes of the other side to get to know the tricks being played to milk the banking system and then leave them high and dry. Thanks to crooked government agencies, I had to take VRS and chose to move overseas, where the corporates are away from the prying eyes of the local Indian system and avoiding direct visibility to all and sundry.

I was posted as chief executive officer of a bank in Hong Kong in mid-2010. It was challenging as well as a great learning experience. In fact, I was already stationed in Hong Kong since the end of 2008 in the same capacity in an organisation under the management of the bank. It was a trade finance outfit regulated by the Hong Kong Monetary Authority (HKMA). Really, it was a small set-up vis-à-vis exposure I had in the bank but the right place to understand policy matters and interactions with regulators in Hong Kong and China on a one-to-one basis while working as the CEO of the bank.

International banking is definitely different from what we do in banks in India. The concepts are totally different, and work is totally professional. The attitude change is immediately visible once you step in this kind of set-up. Each and every one has ears for you, and the credit for this will definitely go to the local staff who are less knowledgeable but far ahead in commitment to their work. The regulatory authorities are interacting with you regularly with straight and pointed observations. Small lapses also get noticed quickly.

PART I

CHAPTER 1

My Various Stints in a Bank

Let us take the journey from the start since December 1983. The then PM had announced a scheme for self-employment for educated youth – a government-sponsored scheme with small loans up to INR 25,000 or 35,000. Congress workers along with all opportunists/ serious candidates all over the country clamoured for the loan. Stiff annual targets were given to all the nationalised banks. Private banks were not there at that time. Along with this, there were other simultaneous schemes for SC/ST, rural areas. The 'Garibi Hatao' slogan was going around. All horses were let loose to make the scheme successful.

In any government directed scheme, the government agencies get involved in identification and recommendation of loans. In the above cases, it was district industries centres and block-level employees of the state government in various other departments. Everyone knows the credibility of these departments. Almost all the applicants were milked by these departments before the applications reached the banks. Against the target of x, 5x applications were sent with full recommendations for loan sanction.

With applicants not being guided properly on the banking requirement of KYC, pre-sanction inspections and project assessment were a big nuisance to bank officers. The process of final loan approval to disbursement is definitely time consuming, and it was much tougher during those days when every step was manual. At many places, the bank staff also became greedy, but thankfully, witch-hunting was less. However, since the origin of the loan process was starting through a corrupt channel, majority of the start-ups failed miserably, and ultimately, banks had to write off loans in five years. In some cases, criminal cases were filed against loanees who vanished immediately upon disbursement of loan. Some parents took the loan in the name of their daughters and got them married with no project initiated. Forget recovery in such cases as no one will share the whereabouts of the married girl after loan disbursement.

Similar were the situations where SC/ST or IRDP schemes were processed. These became more of personal consumer loans but were definitely better than the above scheme.

Branches were very active in financing agricultural equipment like pump set and tractor/accessories. Dealers would offer cuts to bank agricultural officers. Most of them fell for it in semi-urban and rural areas. Honest staff would not fall, but it looked like many definitely fell for this trap and favoured the dealer.

Luckily, I escaped clean from the initial exposure as it seemed like petty theft. However, I was exposed first to fraudulent deals in one credit account wherein a party was forwarding the goods through railways and obtained secured finance against these invoices/ Railway Receipts (RRs) under a bill discounting facility. It was a clear case of cheating which went to CBI, and FIR was filed sometime in the year 1986–87. To my surprise, I was called as witness sometime in 2001 – after fifteen years. I do not know what the judgement was, but I can say that the then borrower must have attained the age of 65–70 years by the time the court would have announced its judgement.

I will touch on investigating agencies and the legal system separately to bring to light their flat-footed, half-hearted approach towards bankers and the probable reasons.

In the next stint as manager of a rural branch, I could see the plight of rural people at the hands of the block-level staff of the state government, and to some extent, gram pradhan, particularly the people from backward classes. These staff members would take 20–25 per cent from each government-related scheme loans with guidance that there was no need to return the loans. However, where land was charged for loan, the borrower would cry as he had to ensure that his land was not sold by default.

Here again, I would say that with positive approach from complete staff guidance to block authorities, we took the onus of selecting borrowers under the government scheme from our field staff's hands, bringing a huge improvement in loan fund use and recoveries, and the bank branch got good reviews all around in its command area. Government agencies also found that things were working fine. Luckily, majority of the staff was young with lots of motivation to help the downtrodden.

I initiated one police action against one borrower related to my predecessor's tenure. Police took its own time to file a case, but I was surprised one night when I got a call from one colleague saying that the court had issued a warrant against me in the year 1996, eight years after filing of the case, for non-appearance as witness. I was shocked at the approach of our bank/ branch manager and the court. Then I initiated support from the bank to appoint a lawyer to take care of the requirements. It looks like the matter died a natural death in court as there was no follow-up thereafter.

In 1988, I moved to a big city centre branch in Allahabad. It was a highly unionised branch with a bad track record. Corruption was at all levels – from sub-staff and clerks to some of the senior officers. However, the bank suddenly woke up, and some of the guilty ultimately got punished, leading to some sanity in the branch. Yes, it was an eye-opener in some areas about how the corrupt thrive with support from various stakeholders within the bank. A four-year term here guided me better as it was my first time being exposed to the conduct of forex, credit business, and various kinds of audits in the branch. Some good officers also suffered in their career because of this audit. I feel sorry for them. It was definitely a good exposure from learning, management, and managing staff relations.

In 1992, I moved to Ghaziabad, a really unhealthy centre for the bank. In fact, my more than three years in the region made me feel that corrupt people were vying to head as the bank's branch manager. The role of the officer's association and their preferred officers were really visible. Those who indulged might have made a small fortune, but majority of these officers suffered heavily in their career as some had to lose their job, while majority lost their career and reputation. To sum it up, risk management – which we study and follow in our work – is applicable to people's work also. Once such officers get entangled in departmental enquiries, the association role becomes the defender to save the job rather than get a clean chit.

Since I was in the main branch without any designation, it was easy for me to move freely within the branch for work and routinely interact with customers. The then incumbent head was easy to succumb; coupled with corrupt team members and infighting between them, things were quite bad. Again, good sense prevailed in the bank, and the fighting officers were moved within six months of my joining. Thereafter, the branch had two highly honest branch heads who brought about overall sanctity in the work.

After a peaceful period in 1995-96 as a manager in the semi-urban branch of Kannauj, a famous historical city, I was moved to Lucknow in 1997 as chief officer of credit in the zonal office. Thankfully, with good bosses around and good teamwork, we were able to take the work to better levels and ensured satisfaction from all clients, small or big – staff loans being approved on the same day or within twenty-four hours. The five-year period of working in the controlling office was quite rewarding with promotion to senior management grade and a significantly important posting to the bank's number one business branch – Mumbai corporate – in early 2002.

In April 2002 to mid-2007, the Mumbai corporate banking branch was having the who's who of the Indian corporate world as its clients such as Reliance, the Tatas, the Birlas, Godrej, Essar, Crompton, government PSUs, and a large number of upcoming corporates to name a few. This was the most happening place, and almost everything moved with the consent of the top management or, to be more candid, at their direction. You can see the egos and fancies of the top management duly supported by corrupt government machinery and politicians ruling the process of credit sanctions/disbursements. Exchange of gratification through various ways could be sensed in majority of the cases at the top, barring some cases of top corporates that were run purely professionally.

Top management people got the bank of their choice through manipulation of political and Ministry of Finance officials, and some corporates played their role with their connections in the corridors of power. Lobbying of all sorts happened, including money exchange or quid pro quo, to get a favourable position when the corporate was involved with some misunderstanding. It was purely dependent on how much help can be given to their supported clients/corporates. It was scratching each other's back so that all remained happy. Government and CA directors were calling the shots in the board of directors' affairs, with some chairman having very little control over them. The appointment came through the government with tacit understanding. Some of the top executives also played into the hands of such board members for furtherance of their career. Some talented and honest executives (GMs) would work in important positions just to ensure that they continued to be in the important portfolio and be known and counted. Despite their honesty, they continued to play into the hands of such board members to retain the important position in the top hierarchy. (Our erstwhile prime minister is a living example of this kind of working relation.) Yes, the boss culture thrives in our Indian banking system.

You can see the true colours of the bank's top management in big loan dispensation. Some big corporates would get a big loan at the drop of a hat, or some would get accommodation funds for huge amounts which would be swindled within a short period. There were a good number of such cases which led to the downfall of some executives who then left the bank and took lucrative assignments through the connections developed through their positions.

Between 2002 and 2007, I saw and observed the work of top management at the Mumbai corporate branch. It sometimes felt surprising that our bank was always the blue-eyed boy of southern politicians, bureaucrats who mattered, and bankers who wished to come to this bank. The plus point with our bank was its good working culture, a better talent pool among PSU banks, and, to top it all, a wide network of overseas branches across the globe. If the history of the bank was observed in the last thirty to forty years, then one would find that it had more south India–based chairmen and managing directors vis-à-vis the people from the place where the bank originated. There are no marks for guessing about who called the shots and how things shaped up in the bank with people whose interest lay beyond banking. Most of these people at the top had left a bad legacy with few exceptions who were concerned with their image.

The aftermath of my predecessor's legacy was felt down the line when cover-up operations were done by people part of the cycle. Many had to face various investigations from internal and external agencies, although they were not involved. Sometimes minnows who were involved in routine operations post-disbursement and hardly had any reason for big loans going bust got prosecuted. The cases that went to investigating agencies of the government of India more or less died a natural death as nothing would come out because protection was extended behind the scenes. I would explain this during the course of this report. These top-level functionaries got patronage for the favours extended and enjoyed a king-sized life once out of position.

All at top management have some favourite corporate groups. After coming out of the bank and working from within the corporate groups overseas, I am able to see how these people have worked to create situations for misuse of bank finance or help make the balance sheet and work look very strong. Resultantly, banks lend more and more until the burden of servicing debt becomes non-viable, making the ship sink under its own weight.

In Maharashtra, it is a well-known fact that any real estate project has to get the green signal from top political heads of various parties first. The game here is simple. It looks like that political heavyweight will induct his crony as one of the minority shareholders in the project company – normally, a Special Purpose Vehicle (SPV) is created for each project – which is mainly coming as sweat equity or small equity funded by the promoters in the name of the crony. The political heavyweight then brings his clout in getting all government approvals so that the project could commence. Once all the approvals fall in place and the project starts, the valuation of the asset goes up. It is when the crony will be allowed exit at a premium without investing.

So many real estate games have come in the open also, but hardly any serious action has been taken by the AML (Anti Money Laundering) authorities. In criminal cases, circumstantial evidence is also taken into account, but that rule is not meant for politicians. I think I will leave this to the imagination of the readers along with various news items they see day to day on the subject as all major cities in the country will be working under the same kind of set-up.

CHAPTER 2

Face to Face with Real Corruption, 2007–8

Real action and exposure to corruption and its magnitude came in May 2007 onwards. In fact, what I saw in eighteen months of my career in the bank on the negative side was equal to my entire service of twenty-four years by that time. In 2007, I was promoted to Asst General Manager grade and transferred as branch head of the mid-corporate branch of the bank in the country's capital city. In the same period, the bank saw change of guard at the top/CMD. Delhi also saw a change of head with a new person coming in as GM. To top it all, the bank also got a new chartered accountant director appointed by the government of India. Both these people at the top had strong political bosses from the government. Both held important positions in the government of the day.

Both the board-level appointees had their own agenda, as well as their masters. Both were permanent members of the management committee, which exercised the lending or financial powers. Since both were there for a limited period, they did not waste time in the achievement of their personal goals/milestones in amassing wealth. The Delhi GM was instructed to fully support the CA director in his agenda of making money. The reason was that this CA director can put a spoke in all credit decision coming for approval at the board level. The top management cannot afford board-level issues. Firstly, he was drawing his strength on his proximity to his political boss; and secondly, being a CA, he had to be a permanent part of the management committee. There were two top politicians who were more powerful in the government of the day.

The action was started immediately by both of them in their field. While a CA director, he was not supposed to interfere in any of the activities of the bank due to conflict of interest at operational level, but he started bringing clients to the bank, and majority of the branch managers in Delhi were directly instructed by the GM to take care of him. The GM confided in a few AGM/DGMs what indications he had from top management and was advised that this annoyance had to be avoided for obvious reasons. We, at branch level, had a tough call to take; and at my level, I shared the information with my whole team about why we would be taking up any new business brought in by him. I made it very clear to officers that they had to be more professional in their approach in respect of cases brought in by the director concerned. Fortunately, we always avoided direct contact with him and avoided his clients, but he would get the GM to pass on the message. Yet he was able to bring a few corporate clients in our bank, which I understand became NPA in two years' time. He would boast of his proximity to his political bosses and would take his cut from the referred cases approved by the branches.

Another fact was that he would contact clients whose papers were going to be presented in the management committee. I am sure many other CA directors on the board of directors of banks would be doing the same for furtherance of their interest. I clearly remember when the bank credit department had introduced one page in the format of credit proposals to bring out the name of key people and their telephone numbers and similar information.

However, these board members proved deadly for the bank as I could notice that all lobbies (consultants, bureaucrats, politicians, corporates) became so active as if there was free distribution. The very first case from this director brought my entire life's hard work to nil. I will narrate a few cases which will help you understand the nexus.

Case 1 – Bank's director nexus: In end of May (say, within fifteen days of my taking charge at the branch), he brought one case for takeover of one call centre (100 per cent export oriented) borrower account from SBI to our bank. As stated above, the GM called me in his cabin in the presence of the director that so-and-so would come and that it had to be done. Accordingly, officers down the line were instructed to be ready. In fact, the prospective client came on the same day, and they were asked to send us a formal request for preliminary examination. It took hardly a short time for the client to give the papers, and phone calls from the director had started coming for the quickest disposal. We did all pre-sanction formalities, and the GM sanctioned the facilities for about ten crores of rupees. Once sanctioned, the director pushed for disbursement as his fee was linked to the funds released to the client. We did our best, but the disbursing officers committed some operational mistakes which even the concurrent auditor (in-house senior officer) could not bring to our notice. This account became quick mortality in less than one year due to internal and external reasons.

In between this, the borrower's parent company also took a corporate loan against a full security of about twenty crores which also became NPA, together with the above. Both units were active call centres. The borrowers definitely had diverted funds overseas, but another reason for failure was the global financial crisis in 2007–8, which had a big impact on Indian call centre units, leading to contracts getting cancelled from overseas clients.

The resultant loss caused heavy damage to the officers who had processed the application. Some complaint happened, which was handled by CBI, ACB, who recommended three officers, including myself, as negligent on procedures. Procedures were already thrown to winds by the bank itself when bosses routinely intruded on the board members. The CBI investigator did not go into any real investigations and did the cut-paste job from banks' internal audit report which was duly taken on record by the committee on internal audit. I was never contacted for any statement during the course of the investigation and was suo motu made the culprit of procedural lapses. Per my knowledge, HO avoided my presence before CBI as I was posted abroad during the period when the investigation was being carried out. While the director/GM and the officer who committed operational mistakes were allowed to go free, we three officers had our career finished and got major penalty despite the departmental enquiry finding exonerating me. No investigation report was shared on which charge sheet was made. CVC insisted on punishment, and I pursued the bank's vigilance/CVC officials to send their recommendations so that I can leave the job. The youngest officer was so badly hurt that he decided to simply not take any future interest in the career, though he was definitely competent to rise to the GM level.

This director was instrumental in three to four accounts at our large corporate branch wherein a consortium of banks lost almost 2,000 crores (group already under investigation). My tough stance on one occasion angered him, leading to my GM telling me to go to the client's office and say sorry. I did that honourably, but the client made me wait for the meeting for almost one hour. He would boast of his proximity to the top political man with whose blessing he was there on the board of the banks. He had the audacity to use our branch meeting room to discuss his business with prospective clients or would walk in without any notice, causing disturbance in routine or meetings under way at the branch with clients/officers. Once, he was seriously ill and admitted in some hospital but would keep calling at odd hours to follow up his recommended cases.

Unfortunately, at the instance of our then superiors, including top management, we did not name him in our replies to the charge sheet/enquiry proceedings.

Simply naming him would have saved the career of officers who suffered. In one of the other branches in Delhi wherein he had gotten a loan sanctioned, the then AGM of the branch named the director in his explanation, which helped him save himself and also get his future promotions. This was just a small indication of the nexus between the CA director and the top management (looter being protected). It was a well-known fact in the branch what mainly caused the failure, but the CBI investigator found a desk job and copied the contents as its report and recommending procedural lapse and major penalty proceedings.

The funny part was more relevant when the officer whose fault made the bank lose the security of ECGC was given a caution as he reported oversight due to being overbusy in routine work. The concurrent auditor who was doing 24/7 audit of the daily routine at the branch was not at all questioned.

Case 2 – Political nexus: This was a small-value loan of six crores of rupees done by three banks jointly (i.e. share of two crores of rupees per bank). All rules were bent to help this loan be awarded to a wilful defaulter. To top it all, this was approved by the whole board as it contravened all policy norms of the bank/RBI. Would you believe who were all trying to help this loan account whose factory was located in

Amethi (no guessing whose constituency)? Apparently, the borrowing person was a front for some bigwig or someone very near and dear to them. All the three banks sanctioned and disbursed two crores of rupees each, which was approved by the whole board as it was being given to a defaulter whose name appeared in the RBI defaulter list.

With so much double standard on procedural lapses, I found it most amusing that when I returned to India as zonal manager of Delhi, I found the name of the person as defaulter as he did not pay any single penny to the bank in four years. When I called the person for a follow-up meeting on the loan repayment (HO was after zone to improve recovery in big accounts which were the direct responsibility of the zonal manager) and during the course of discussion, he started telling stories. When we pressed hard on this person, our chairman/ED got a call from the FS not to bother this person. Thus, this reached a dead end.

Case 3 – Top management nexus: Just touching two cases here as majority of his cases were handled at the large corporate branch (both branches in the same building [i.e. ground floor and first floor]), and we did get to know what is going on in both branches. The large corporate branch was more active in real estate loans of builders who were in the news for all the wrong reasons these days, with majority of the promoters behind bars or under deep stress. All these were either through consultants or directly with the principal promoters.

One Z group was sanctioned a loan for takeover of an SBI loan for his steel plant in Bihar. The promoter discussed with the CMD and GM, and Mumbai called to submit the proposal immediately. I think we did not have time to process and submitted papers based on the information provided by the borrower. The proposal was approved within a few days, and the loan was sanctioned for takeover of the SBI liabilities. The same person was given more than 100 crores or rupees in Mumbai. Understand that this group caused loss of more than 2,200 crores of rupees to the banking sector in India. CBI, ED, and Serious Fraud Investigation Office are pursuing the case (ha ha ha!), but all seems eyewash as nothing is reported on the update.

This was the story of the people who had been given the responsibility to protect the very foundation of the institution, but these very people were eating the foundation like there is no other day to live. They thrived in their quest for money. In fact, if our regulatory and investigation agencies were good enough, everything could have come out in the open about the deeds going on in these two years.

I fail to understand why the top man who was instrumental in huge fraudulent loan sanctions has not been booked till date. If the GM/EDs of that period are interrogated under lie detector, full details of who were involved can be brought to light. Because of his political support, investigations are so slow, and nothing is being done. I am sure greasing of hands at all levels is being done by the corporates on their behalf.

To top it all, if the linked people engaged in the investigation are put to the real test, then one will know how our government investigating agencies work. Their investigation is so slack towards the real culprit, while the smaller people who performed their duties at the behest of bosses get penalised. With the amount involved, one can imagine what role a small officer could have played.

During 2007–9, he was more often seen in Chennai and overseas. No need to guess why Chennai visits were important. It was known in the bank that the top political man's son had been frequenting many bank headquarters in Mumbai as he was also running an advisory outfit. His Master's Voice was very important to him.

Bureaucratic Intervention: IAS lobby in the Indian system rules the banking sector with its invisible hands. I have seen their role from behind the scenes on various occasions and also from the front. It depends on the daring qualities the person has.

In the initial years, IAS from Financial Services, GoI were appointed as directors to actively attend board meetings, particularly the management committee, that sanctioned loans. Slowly, they found out that fire was touching them also due to reckless consideration of loans where all the crooked were involved to make a fortune at the cost of public money. They then moved back behind the scenes and controlled their interest.

One such gentleman was the blue-eyed boy of most of the top management of banks as he used to protect and lobby for them in the ministry. He was actively pursuing loan sanctions for his favourite corporates, with his younger brother acting as consultant in Delhi. Here again was the same process. The GM would call you in his chamber in front of the gentleman brother, and instructions were issued. Needless to say, these people had no interest in the loss to the bank. They needed their cut, and the rest was with the corporate client who already had his plans when to run away with the bank money.

My experience further showed that even a small clerk in FS in Delhi has got the guts to come to the bank once any client meets some IAS and goes through this clerk with the purpose known. He will share his number to let him know about the progress/approval.

There are no guesses to be made in understanding the clout this section of bureaucracy enjoys and controls the PSU Banks in influencing financial decisions for their favour corporates or even new corporates.

International loans, 2007–09: One such case was in Hong Kong. The top man was notified to take over from his then bank to ours. He had a favourite client who was setting up a compact disc unit in Rajasthan and was given good support by him from his previous bank. This client was also operating from Dubai. Whatever may have been the reason for starting a trading unit in HK, the incoming top man told the then international GM to sanction this guy's credit facilities in HK. The GM could pursue the then CMD and start with US$2.5 million. The moment he took over, the credit facilities were enhanced to US$5 million and then to US$10 million all within six months' time. No procedure lapses, just whim and fancy. Thereafter, he did not pay any money to the bank; and to avoid quick mortality, the new top management released a cash margin to keep the account floating for a few more months. With his background, he had gotten this person credit lines from a few other banks in HK also, and all had to take full loss.

The bank needs to carry out a study of loans sanctioned during his time to understand his favourite spot for extending favours both in Indian and international centres. The diamond industry was also a favourite stop, and a recent big-name defaulter was also favoured in China. Needless to say, this was also a lost case. Similarly, many groups would come to knowledge provided by investigating authorities and get the right people from within the bank to expose his designs. This man was more than pleased to serve his boss besides another superior boss, money.

This top person of the bank is being investigated for over ten years, and still, our Indian investigating agencies like CBI, SFIO, and ED are just dragging their feet. Some of the officers who were signatories to these proposals are shuttling between these agencies with no result. The competence of our investigating agencies can be seen daily from the newspaper or heard through the grapevine.

Similar was the case with the successor top man in 2009–12. He was less reckless but had his own agenda. He also brought his favourite clients from previous banks. Big names appearing in the news also got a small start in HK and maybe elsewhere. What followed may be in the knowledge of our government agencies that remain in deep slumber.

The bank had a first lady top person for three years in about 2012 till mid-2015. She had started her shopping the moment she landed in the chair. All-round development of brokers improved during her tenure both in domestic and international markets. She milked the bank to her best and cultivated some top executives who were ambitious to scale new heights as ED/CMD. Needless to say, this lady also left a bad legacy of big non-performing assets.

One incident during her tenure comes to mind. She had taken charge of the bank and had called on FS (GOI) in October/November 2012. Upon her return, she came to the zonal office and said that the FS's wife was going to Bangkok with some friends and that the FS had asked her to arrange cash for her at the Bangkok airport. She asked me to arrange this as I had recently come from Hong Kong and can manage this. I told her that one PSU bank had a branch in Bangkok and that she can tell the CMD of that bank who would be more than happy to grant the FS's wishes. She did not agree and said, 'I have told the FS that this will be done, and now you find ways.' In front of her, I called the Chief Eexecutive in HK and told him to fly to Bangkok and get US$5,000 worth of Thai baht delivered to the wife of the FS at the airport. This gentleman complied and then had to confirm to the CMD/FS (mobile number was shared) once the assignment was satisfactorily concluded. This gentleman subsequently reached the top position of our bank, an indication of how low our bosses and government top functionaries work for self-benefit.

Another incident comes to mind about her initial period in the bank. She told us (General Manager and Zonal Manager) that she was sending one reference for a big importer of coal for about 300 crore of rupees. We suggested that the client be sent to our large corporate branch in Delhi, which she straight away refused, and she instructed that this be handled by some other big branch in the same city. No choices with such top management people. The head office processed and sanctioned, and the branch disbursed. Thankfully, by the time this disbursement process was done, I was transferred to the head office in Mumbai. Later on, I learned that the facilities of 375 crores of rupees have turned NPA, and fraud investigation has been given to the government agencies. It is understood that the account was done at the behest of some top functionaries of government of that day.

I also saw her role in a big fraudulent account, which is coming in the second part of this study. Personal agenda overtook the reality in this case. Hence, instead of arresting the problem, she helped in further escalating losses to the bank she was heading. The irony of the matter is that the very same group accounts are under probe by authorities for fraud and money laundering. However, the role of top management of various banks is not being put to the real test.

The motivation and final decision to move out came during various interactions at the head office and finally sometime in early 2014 when I was attending one management committee board Meeting wherein all financial and credit matters are approved. It was a big credit proposal where severe default was already visible, and even the best-case scenario was not in a position to restore the business back on track in the foreseeable future. However, the Chair person was not willing to take this big NPA of over Rs.1000 crores in the Bank with similar impact of huge losses to other consortium member banks. All procedures and policy guidelines were being thrown to the winds to keep this problem out during her tenure.

All banker friends are aware of evergreening or resorting to steps to avoid the reporting of NPAs and also managing statutory auditors to avoid reporting of NPAs as long as possible. As a regular handler of credit matters, including large credit for almost thirty years in the bank, we have been through all these matters at all places. Majorly, this is done per instructions from the top, and reality remains under the carpet. Most of the branch managers also resort to this under-reporting as it is forming part of the performance indicator. It is also a fact that **PSU** banks do not have adequate manpower to follow up on loan accounts properly, and only when things go out of control does firefighting start to salvage the situation.

PART II

CHAPTER 3

Other Side of the Coin
(Corporate World Overseas)

This period belongs to my entry on the corporate world of Indian promoters having business in the overseas market. These promoters are sharp and know how to make quick money through bad means instead of more genuine business. This I came to know from 2014 onwards. With the amount of goodwill I enjoyed among clients, I got a good response on my re-entry into Hong Kong for my second professional inning. I have fully encashed this goodwill to infiltrate their citadel. You can say that I became a mole in their system.

I had been through severe stress since 2009 due to issues related to banking which made me leave the bank and take a new assignment overseas with the hope that things would improve in my personal life. However, once in Hong Kong, people whom we trusted as a banker taught me tricks of their trade. Slowly, I started to see the true colours of these very people. Then it struck my mind to get deeper into the various games these people played. I definitely tried to warn the Indian system on two occasions, but you cannot enjoy half-baked cake. The truth and facts have to be substantiated with evidence, and in the Indian system, a person speaking the truth is sometimes made to suffer or forced to lie low. As said elsewhere, I have nothing more to gain from the bank, but I'm making my new knowledge public so that the system can benefit out of it. This time, it is based on facts and evidence.

While working in Hong Kong during 2008 to 2012, I had gained good exposure in international trade, arbitrage, and commodity trade. The reason apparently was working on international structured trade finance wherein interest arbitrage was a major attraction. Many Indians were involved from India, Hong Kong, Singapore, and Dubai in this trade. Most of these Indians had floated multiple entities at these centres with full control of funds. The post-Lehman-collapse market was highly liquid, but the Indian system was still highly attractive on deposit interest rates. Besides, Indian banks in the overseas market had their own problem in raising low-cost funds. Resultantly, Indian PSU banks were offering much better rates in USD than counter MNC banks. This helped the banks in raising one-year funds easily, and deployment thereof in matching assets was proving quite beneficial.

The above situation allowed a huge number of HK entities as well as overseas entities to foray into interest arbitrage by placing deposit and opening trade Letter of Credits for 360 days. The trade was duly backed by supporting trade documents like Air Way Bill, BL, or warehouse receipt. At my bank, after I took over as CE in HK and studied the asset portfolios of peer banks locally, we found this as a big opportunity for profits through treasury operation and also building steady trade assets and earn good income with zero risk as the exposure was fully covered by deposit or bank acceptance to pay on due date. Coupled with this, there was an advantage on fee-based income and also clients maintaining their current account balance. This helped bring down the cost of operations substantially.

This high-volume letter of credit business was also giving goosebumps, which I always felt whether this much consumption is happening in the world or not. Nevertheless, since full security was available, we carried on the business with full caution and complete control on papers. We used to have regular discussion with our core team at the branch so that everyone knew what was being done and how the mind was working to ensure full safety and compliance to bank, HKMA, and RBI policies.

In no time, our bank was leading among all PSU banks, with a team of officers and local staff fully supporting the business through quick services/disposal of various requests. During this period, we also pushed the local staff to bring Chinese clients for deposits, which proved very good as getting interest on deposit at 2–3 per cent per annum was unheard of by the local Chinese community. They placed deposits happily to the extent of government protection available to them. The number of such depositors continued increasing. The benefit can be gauged from the financial results of the centre, which doubled in one year time from the budgeted levels even after providing for bad debts.

The best part was bonhomie among all Indian officers and their families and also with the local staff who were rewarded with good annual increments. Majority of the Indian officers due for promotion were also highly recommended for promotion at the time of interviews. Luckily, efforts made duly resulted in a fruitful outcome for the aspiring officers to higher grades, a rare achievement for the centre. Majority of these officers are now general managers in the bank. I am sure a good future awaits them as they are still young to compete for higher levels in the remaining time of their service.

Post-repatriation to India, I found that some clients from Singapore and India were keen to have association with me, and full feelers were there to leave the job and join them in Hong Kong for their new office. The major choice was between two groups, one from UK and the other from Singapore. The Singapore promoter offered a better term in the form of partnership, while the UK group was not committing financially on certain things for working in Hong Kong. It seemed a challenge to work more independently in structure with the Singapore group promoter, who was regularly pursuing personal meetings on a couple of occasions in Mumbai also.

I already had a couple of good opportunities in Mumbai while I was working there. I would have derived more than what I was getting in the bank. I then took one opportunity in Mumbai and the other in Hong Kong with the condition that if I did not succeed in the international market, then I can come back. There is no doubt that I had adequate exposure in the bank in the areas of credit, forex, international trade documentation, and dealing with banks and the outside business community in developing business with full trust and confidence.

Once I stepped into the business world of the Indian promoters and finance experts, I observed that the basic trait in being successful is the art of sweetly lying to the person in front of you. All types of lies ranging from business to finance to family matters will be spoken to make the listener become compassionate and fall in the trap.

HONG KONG STRUCTURE AS AN ENTREPRENEUR

Hong Kong, Singapore, and UAE are the most attractive financial and trading centres in Asia with very little oversight from regulators for the trading community. All these centres host the big names in the trading world in one form or the other as Asia continues to be the busiest place for manufacturing and consumption due to continued development. The idea of the association was to create companies in my name (joint venture [JV] behind the scenes) with all the business initially generated through Singapore team effort, and slowly, I can create new opportunities for JV in Hong Kong. The business backbone was arbitrage on international trade. Once I informed him about tentative dates of my joining his scheme of things in early April 2014, he had made an arrangement for the formation of companies in Hong Kong as well as offshore companies. I visited Singapore first to meet him and get his plan, but the starting point was to focus on arbitrage for his business-related companies, and I would be developing local clients as well. Hong Kong was always a very good centre for this kind of business.

However, the story behind this slowly started unfolding to me when I landed in my personal capacity and not as a banker, a very creative way of manipulating the banking system by Indians. (I had little access to locals in HK.)

Before moving to HK, the Singapore group had finalised four companies, two HK-based companies and two offshore (British Virgin Islands/Seychelles). The understanding was that, after all operative expenses, I would be getting 10 per cent of the profit. These companies had me as a single shareholder director in two companies and 90 per cent in another company initially with the Singapore promoter's known person. The third company with major shareholding under the Singapore person control was to do bigger volumes. Definitely, this was done by Singapore employer with an eye on checking on my capabilities to run the affairs or otherwise control would have been wrested by him with majority shareholding being under his nominated person's control. Fair. Any new person will work with a lot of diligence in a totally new relationship. This shareholding structure was changed fully in my name as of 31 March 2015 with increase in paid-up capital to ten million HKD, which was required to have an investor visa in Hong Kong.

Offshore companies are floated in most of the financial centres to avoid the eyes of local tax authorities and save taxes in the normal course, but in reality, this majorly helps hide the relationship with the fund movement as the origination of fund changes to a different country. More details will come in due course when the specific transaction will be explained.

All companies were successfully accepted by banks for new account except BVI as this had become very noticeable in the eyes of regulators for laundering. The Singapore team immediately worked on another offshore company through Seychelles with me as sole shareholder and director, which also found favour with banks. Further, since I was an ex-CEO of a big Indian bank in HK and was going to bring a good volume of LC-backed trades, it was easy to have an account with all the local Indian banks. Thus, the launching pad was made ready to start Hong Kong operations in June– July 2014.

CHAPTER 4

Modus Operandi – Genesis of Corrupt Practices

BANKING – STRUCTURED BALANCE SHEET

As a banker, we have always been guided to understand the balance sheets of the client before taking credit decisions. The bigger the lending requirement, the keener the scrutiny of the financial results of the borrower. Even new venture projections have to be put to rigorous scrutiny before being accepted and arriving at a financing decision. During trainings, we are told to be guided by the saying 'Please crunch the numbers, and the numbers would speak for themselves.' Perfect for ideal conditions. However, this is not true anymore in the present business climate. The experience which was gained during banking is totally different from reality. My experience is totally based on Indian clients who were subjects of my association in an overseas set-up. However, similar things hold true for Indian business when I go back to memory lane to see what we did during our long time working in credit functions of the bank at various levels. An exception to the rule is always there, but in majority of cases, truth will range from 50 to 80 per cent, and the rest will be created to satisfy the bank.

During the period of late 1990s to early 2000, the Indian banking sector saw an emergence of new technology-savvy banks like ICICI Bank, Axis Bank, and IDBI Bank. The emergence also brought new financial terminologies like *structured finance*, *financial engineering*, *financial derivatives*, and so on. It took time to match the young generation's control on marketing, but finally, PSU banks lost a lot of ground in the SME/mid-segment. These banks employed good marketing techniques with delivery of services through a digital platform combined with sale of exotic financial and foreign exchange products to the targeted segment, which mostly boomeranged on them. The entire game was based on a future which the best cannot foresee. Lots of people lost huge monies and found themselves at the receiving end, facing extinction. This did not last beyond 2010, when things started unfolding.

The emergence of new generation banks gave rise to new ideas to clients as they saw that maximum banking decisions are based on financials. The borrowing clients and corporates found new ways to get quick money through the use of new generation people. Both had interest in quick money. This led to the emergence of *structured balance sheets*. The adopted way was simple and also planned with time horizon in mind.

These high-flying corporates and borrowers started fudging the financial results. This was the era of creating false sales invoices to jack up the top and bottom lines. Then came setting up of companies through which these sales and purchases would be routed. This idea requires full awareness of how to manipulate balance sheets and create a web of companies to hold the shares and still maintain control – an idea often deployed by big corporate promoters. Then there would be actual movement of funds shown through the bank accounts. It is planned in such a way that the new balance sheet meets all the banking sector requirements for extending the finance. In a couple of years, balance sheets will appear to be fine, though profits may not be shown very high as it makes tax liabilities go up. This is more easily achieved in trading companies. Manufacturing units also manipulate but have less manoeuvrability. Yet they will start showing trading sales also to justify the increase in sales. Majority of these entry provider companies are held in the name of employees or insignificant people who, once exposed, will be told to go away or become untraceable. Their integrity can be bought for small sums or through threats.

A closer scrutiny of default accounts with the banks will show the trend. RBI, in particular, and regulators all over will have to put a research team to study such defaulted account financial results. Even these defaulting borrowers will show legal notices and actions to show that they have done their part in realisation.

Once the desired balance sheet is achieved, the borrowing unit approaches the bank. From down to up, everyone is happy with the financials as the same has been audited, which puts his authenticity to the results. The ball is rolling, and as a banker, we fall for the good accounts to grow our asset portfolio and earn to improve its bottom line. All is fair till it lasts – death comes in the next five years upwards if further support is not extended.

(This I will prove with the creation I have done myself without putting in any serious money.)

STRUCTURED CREDIT RATING

The goal of good financials is achieved, with the figures appearing in the books of accounts. There is now a bank requirement to call for credit rating. India has now a number of rating agencies. However, outside India, bankers do not insist on rating for unlisted corporates. Here, Dun & Bradstreet's or some similar organisation's assessment on risk appetite is accepted. The Indian banking sector accepts this report on an importer/exporter about the legitimacy of the parties dealing with the system.

It is well known that credit rating agencies do a good analysis on the numbers reflected in the audited financials and also call for various other information. However, here is the catch. They do not know that the promoter has been working on the figures for two to three years before it is taking the big step. In the manufacturing units, the manipulation is less, but they are also doing their bit to keep things rosy till banking support is available. Manufacturing has some limitation as production and industry data can be verified, and cross-checks are available. As mentioned in earlier lines, there are ways to grow top line/bottom line for them to also keep things under the carpet.

Trading outfits do not fall in this category. They are free to work on the figures, provided some surplus cash is available with the promoter. He has already created enough number of sellers and buyers (apart from actual). These funds' routing help in top/bottom line for making a credible balance sheet. Bottom line is the least important for trading units as it is justified that those quick sales and purchases are done, and marginal profit is booked. To add to their balance sheet, there are enough number of entry providers for small percentage gains.

For a credit rating agency, all these structured balance sheets are just good for making quick money, while in reality it is the borrower who is feeding on their report through the banks/lenders. Daring trading units go for public issues also based on ratings obtained through a well-laid road map. Listed companies become more liberal in their spending just to show that new funds are being deployed fruitfully. Again, reality is that the promoter is sweeping funds which are meant for his welfare or some other plans. The names of these companies will appear in specific cases being brought to make the banking fraternity understand the truth lying behind the figures reported. The amount of effort they put in getting the improved credit rating from leading rating agencies will bring doubts on the rating agencies' credibility as their work after an account fails shows that number crunching does not always prove right.

Broadly speaking, various rating models do not serve the purpose unless the balance sheet has brought true figures in public. Again, based on experience overseas and also in India at corporate branches, the extent of truth in financial parameters of trading outfits will be 50 to 80 per cent, and the rest is cooked. Lenders have to take their own view while extending finance to trading units. Manufacturing deserves a little better treatment. Rating agencies produce what is actually fed through books, and the masterminds have planned for them in advance.

STRUCTURED TRADE – INDIAN/INTERNATIONAL LETTER OF CREDIT MONETISATION

Indians are very innovative in financial manipulations. They will find ways to structure trade to suit their requirement. This is something strange but an easy way of raising low-cost funds through bank borrowings and just maintain adequate cash to keep mismatch in check. This I first noticed while I was posted as zonal manager in New Delhi. At that time, I realised how the system was being used. In hindsight, I realised that this was also prevalent in large corporates in Mumbai and in manufacturing and real estate/projects as well as trading. The usance LC facilities are being used depending on the necessity in the business. This is more possible for bigger corporates as well as medium players in all kinds of business lines.

In normal course, the cost of fund-based credit facilities is always higher than non-funded facilities. Based on customers' projections, bankers are more liberal in granting non-funded lines as bankers feel that the goods will be procured through proper means, and cash involvement is less. Also, it helps in the better management of credit facilities, though the income is less for the bank. This holds very good in the Indian market. However, customers have different designs for the use of non-funded facilities as they prefer to have usance lines. The longer the usance lines, the better it is for the customer. The borrowing unit will have, in many cases, its own arranged supplier. Once the documents under LC comes, the bank will be willing to happily discount the LC as the payment is guaranteed by the LC opening bank. The banks are lending under such circumstances around their best lending rates or BPLR or sometimes finer also. Thus, there is a good interest arbitrage of 2 to 3 per cent vis-à-vis the funded line. Besides this, cash generated in associate companies will be available for use when needed. Additionally, LC procurement in actual trade also helps as cash generated through sales can be rotated more than once till the payment for LC is due. The bankers provide an LC facility on the projected cycle of business, whereas in many cases the cycle is much smaller. This holds good for both import and export. Then the buyer credit is used in case of import Documents Against acceptance

LCs to defer the payments and use the cash per their comfort. Buyer credit further helped in hiding the real problems for some time, including helping the bank in arresting slippages.

Now take the instances of few corporates in Mumbai who were running tight on their schedule for their projects, and promoters had to infuse funds. These non-funded facilities helped them a great deal in raising funds as the buyer and the seller were within the group but shown as unrelated parties. In India, arranging paperwork is not difficult. Even if the deal is done genuinely, there are ways to get the cash immediately as there are enough takers for those goods through an understanding. The money thus raised goes to the way the corporate desires. On due dates of LC payment, funds are managed, and all looks great. Book keeping is an art which the corporate accounts and finance team are able to manage without disturbing the management.

In the real estate sector, particularly where construction material is required, the front of supplier of various materials is created in such a way that invoices and deliveries are created to raise funds through working capital lines for construction material suppliers. It is very simple. Then there is another way of seeking funds. Get letter of credit limits for any activity, including exports of garments (mainly Dubai). DA LC is taken for supplies, and goods are shipped with a lot of over-invoicing. Export documents are discounted, and the drawback is claimed from the department. Funds back locally through discounting and are used in real estate projects. On due date, LC is paid. The cycle is safe and complete with no doubts whatsoever.

I made a report to my GM of risk management in late 2012 or early 2013. After seeing my letter which was demi official in nature, the GM called back immediately so as not to put the letter on record. He said that he had deleted the letter from his computer and that I should also do so from my email. In official parlance, any DO letter means that you are bringing the matter directly to the authorities' attention, whereas inter-office memorandum is more public in nature. Involving the boss directly means that he has to take action, which he avoided. Fortunately, I accepted his view at that time as most of the seniors were retiring, and the issue raised would go up to the top management and board, and more scrutiny of the portfolio would be called for. I did not delete the letter from my email as I knew that it may be of use someday. The bank can retrieve it as I think it would still be there on record.

STRUCTURED TREASURY FUNCTIONS

While I was posted in Hong Kong, the interest arbitrage business was growing fast. The exercise was simple. Clients would place a deposit of, say, a few million US dollars for six, nine, twelve or months and, in odd cases, two years. The deposit would be used for opening a fully secured letter of credit – DA/usance matching deposit maturity date. Most of the time, the LC would be covering future interest also to enjoy maximum benefit on the LC issuance. It was a risk-free proposition for a banker which also resulted in fee income. One thing is good – in the overseas market, you can structure each transaction based on the bank's appetite for this kind of business, and matching deployment of funds into India fixed deposit rates vis-à-vis overseas are always very high, and sometimes the differential is quite big, depending on the country where one is investing.

The client would be taking the LC onto a bank which would be willing to discount the trade DA LC at a better interest rate vis-à-vis the deposit rate. Trade transaction under LC would conclude in less than five to seven working days. Post-discounting of the LC, the depositor gets his funds, plus a little profit. This is interest arbitrage simply explained. Many banks are doing this all over the world market where US dollars are cheaply available, and transaction still is profitable. Most of the developed financial centres permit arbitrage of various kinds, including Hong Kong/Singapore. The LC opening bank, mostly Indian PSU/private sector banks, became very active as we found that treasury functions can bring good income to the bank. We would take deposit only after checking whether profitable deployment in the interbank market is available. Very little would be used to cover mismatch. All overseas offices in one country work as an independent unit or a full-fledged bank following local regulations per policies framed. RBI regulations are always there, which are covered in centre-specific policies approved by each bank's board.

Post-Lehman-fiasco in 2008, there was good liquidity in the interbank forex market, and Indians were expanding like anything. Most of our peer banks grew assets under this category, and profits were doubled. The news reached them fast, and Indian HNIs and some corporates having presence in the overseas market also saw a good opportunity in this area. They also generated funds in overseas markets or opened companies in Hong Kong, Singapore, or Dubai to grab this opportunity. These were mostly gold/bullion/jewellery people or commodity traders who were in a position to create a structure backed by underlying assets. With liquidity restored fast, these clients were able to do high volume of trades, resulting in cumulatively high returns annually on one single initial investment in bank deposit. Banks and clients were all fine on account of upward movement in the bottom line and improved percentage in asset quality.

REAL-TIME CASES OVERSEAS

While starting in Hong Kong mainly in an advisory role, to stay in the market, you have to have working companies. So, I had four Hong Kong–registered companies and two offshore companies (BVI/Seychelles), which are already discussed above. These companies were dedicated to clients for structured trade activities as planned by the Singapore group; I was given freedom to add clients for the growing business. The initial flow of business floated from few corporates from Indian groups and thereafter from Singapore, Hong Kong, and UAE or for that matter any other place. This included actual trade too besides structured trade. Structured trade has some actual movement of goods, but reality is different from real trade. The basic aim of the group was to enhance income through arbitrage or monetise. Incidentally, I had good exposure to international structured trade and arbitrage business, which resulted in a good name as a decision taker and faith in my abilities to sustain profits for the bank in Hong Kong.

I wanted to gain knowledge and also be fruitfully engaged. However, it became clear that structured trade in Hong Kong, Singapore, and UAE was quite different. The structured trade done by Indian promoters in the overseas market was quite different from the real structured trade. The practice was brought by Indians who were interested in getting rich overnight. Their idea is to create a balance sheet which helps them raise their finance based on audited returns. In other words, the balance sheets so submitted are doctored with the percentage of actual trade being nominal, while the balance sheet is created with invoices raised between various groups and associated companies which are shown as settled through normal banking channels. Resultantly, no auditor or lender can raise any doubt on this as the bank statements can be verified and willingly offered for verification to give credence to the trading. In fact, most of the balance sheets are a dream so that the bankers fall in the trap. Then this will keep going till the going is good, and the bank raises hands to help them more. Thereafter, debt servicing becomes tough as, so far, it is being done through new funding by the banks. The time now comes for the promoters to fleece or become bankrupt in the overseas market, depending on the situation. A good amount is already parked in safe locations/group companies for continued enjoyment, which the money is capable of bringing to one and sundry.

REAL TIME CASES USED TO TEST

Bankers are made guinea pigs by fraudulent corporate promoters all across the world. Some have big ideas and have started and finished with small games. As a practising banker for over three decades who was more active in larger credit matters in India and the overseas centre, I had become known in the corporate finance business wherever I worked. I am sure people remembered me for my reasonable understanding of business and, above all, for remaining cordial in all situations with promoters and their team. Resultantly, I was able to extract better information and keep a good client/banker relationship. This helped a lot, though people say I am soft and little bit simple.

While taking the call to leave the Bank after seeing the wrongs being done, I took up a new assignment overseas. It was again found that the trust in people is not easy to come and people try to use the experience of a banker to benefit their business more with motive known to them rather than opening up. It became clear, after a few months of working overseas that things need to be seen from within. At this stage it occurred to me that the time has come to commence a study in the wrong practices being practised by Indian corporates in running their business with bank finance and slowly bring this out at appropriate time so that the Banking and finance community derives the benefit of my study. I kept making inroads into the Indian businesses to understand how the wrongs are committed and hopefully this study may ultimately be understood by the regulators and bankers including insurers to save good money. All the study cases took time but I am sure they are worth the wait covered in this study.

CHAPTER 5

The Looters

This part represents some test cases of large value, though there are a good number of cases which were made a subject of this study. Besides, I had been approached by a good number of people from India and some other parts to help them in banking facilities which I tactfully did not undertake as I could see what these people meant while seeking financial facilities from banks in Hong Kong.

Case 1 – Singapore: My first test was the person who engaged me with his perseverance in bringing me to Hong Kong. I had not met him before my posting in Hong Kong, though I had an idea about his business when I was working in Mumbai. We had sanctioned credit lines to his company for the manufacturing of computer motherboards. He once visited Hong Kong during my stay as CE of BOI. Though he did not mention anything, I could sense that he had some offer as he invited me to visit Singapore and see his office. Good for me as I had planned to visit Singapore on my way back to India at the time of repatriation. I paid a visit to his business place sometime in August 2012 while on the way back to India. He had definitely shown good warmth.

Thereafter, he visited India a few times and brought the offer on the table. I was facing a dilemma due to internal issues in the bank as the career was at stake. Other offers were also there for Hong Kong from different big names, but then I decided to go for a known person from Singapore on joint venture terms as, during my Hong Kong posting, something relating to arbitrage trade was not clear, particularly how all Indians were able to create so much trading volume and from where such large sums were available at their disposal.

His office was fully entrenched in helping merchanting trade for two big merchant exporters (India-based group) and some others too on low scale besides also working on arbitrage on his own. Since he was actually into computer products and coal, it was easy for him to generate actual trade bill of lading; and surprisingly, it was generated at the drop of a hat from his end with full tracking of cargo movement. Container tracking is best for the banks to ensure authenticity of the bill of lading. To top it all, it was a freight forwarder bill of lading, which can be generated once the shipment has started by the shipping agent against payment of a small fee. You can keep changing the shipper or connected parties until the cargo is on high seas with the master bill of lading with the shipping line. At the end of the cargo, disposal remains with the master bill of lading holder.

Over a period, it came to my knowledge through unconfirmed sources in Singapore that the bill of lading going to the banks was generated by the shipping agent under his control. All his cargo was mainly going to UAE or sometimes to Nigeria or some other places. India cargo is not permitted under merchanting trade. This helped him corner the maximum business of both the group.

I gave him a long rope to manipulate me according to his wishes, which helped me in getting his mind and his thought process in business. This group had created a huge number of onshore/offshore companies to help merchanting trade parties. He used similar tricks for companies floated in my name. A huge network of companies helped him make good balance sheets on onshore companies in various places. Thereafter, he was pushing for higher and higher credit lines through the banking and trade finance arms operating all over based on balance sheets. Many of these companies were in the name of his employees, but fund use was fully under his control. To top it all, he also introduced some clients to route business through me, which was part of my study hereunder.

While I am finishing this writing about him, he has already duped the system of more than US$200 million through various credit products in his principal company as well as his related companies. I will rate him as the number one money-laundering associate for many Indian clients. His web of companies used for laundering is in various locations but has used his offshore companies well to cover the trail.

His audacity goes to the extent that he called Indian bankers 'pimps' when things went out of control as he was expecting that banks would run after him to settle his dues in his favour with some quid pro quo. His statement is true as he got facilities from various banks with his approach at the top in a few Indian banks over a period.

Case 2 – India: This group is a big name in Uttar Pradesh (Uttar Pradesh) and the family still enjoys the brand name. Unfortunately, I have not met them in person, but it was my first motivation to leave the banking industry. The group was already in deep trouble in 2013 financially, but thanks to throwing all caution to the winds and real banking credit policies, the Indian banking consortium gave a lifeline to ensure that the death did not happen during the time of the then top bosses of the consortium banks. Incidentally, I was present in one such management committee. meeting wherein this arrangement was proposed to defer NPA status. All fell in line for it to pass for some more time till they retired. The writing was on the wall, but additional facilities/release of cash margins resorted to deferring the NPA status.

This group had obtained huge credit lines for merchanting trade over the years from the banking system in India and overseas, but instead of doing factual trade, they moved in interest arbitrage with the non-funded credit lines of the bank through merchanting documents. Bankers know what merchanting trade is in an export-import business, which is also well defined in *Foreign Exchange Management Act* (earlier exchange control manual of RBI). This was going on since 2003–4, and surprisingly, not a single bird opened its mouth – be it branch staff or various auditors, internal or external, statutory or RBI – when it automatically blew itself in 2013 when firefighting started to ensure that top management was able to avoid head rolling in their time. To sum it up, monies were diverted/laundered well before the situation became worse through mismatch in merchanting trade, wherein bank funds were used to create deposit for arbitrage, while the position relating to credit lines remained open. The entire process was camouflaged through various banks used for different categories of business.

Case 3 – India: This group from UP, India, was into commodities and had burnt its fingers in Russia due to exchange rates in ruble when USSR was broken into various countries sometime in 1999–2000. During that time, the bank provided the group restructuring, and they successfully came to life. This was the period when the Indian market was showing a vibrant economy, and new financial products were being sold in the market. Interest arbitrage was one of the biggest tools to make good money through trading activities. This was feasible in the overseas market, and business houses having export/import lines started taking advantage of the low cost of borrowing in the overseas market and placing funds raised in local rupee deposits at high interest rates. In this case, the higher the ability to raise low-cost funds and place a deposit in Indian banks, the better is the margin. It was a volume game. Being in merchanting trade, they were being approached by big commodity players whose main business plan was using business houses which had a foothold in local and overseas markets. The Indian market also saw big international commodity players making their presence in India, and they tried associating with known players in the field for their business. These international players also had new ideas for quick money. Most of these names had huge presence in the Singapore market. The volume game introduced by these people helped companies make big balance sheets which ultimately helped the corporates get good credit lines mostly non-funded from banks in India and overseas through their subsidiaries or front entities.

The greed of such corporates to become big overnight by all means is not unknown. Bankers also fall for good balance sheets to grow. The moment a client becomes big, he stops visiting the branch but directly meets the top bosses. Top bosses in PSU banks, barring exceptions, have different agenda in the company of such ambitious corporates. Majority of the time, they know the real games being played by businesses. Suddenly, credit lines, preferably non-funded, are approved just to show that a genuine business will be transacted.

This was not true in all the three cases here. In merchanting trade, since the goods are not passing through Indian ports, there is no custom inspection. Only the documents, invoices, and bill of lading reach banks, where verification is difficult. In the case of commodity items, prices can be verified to some extent; but in respect of goods of other nature packed in containers, no verification is possible. The bill of lading can declare anything, but inside, the real items are difficult to know. These are declared in a generalised way like computer products, whereas in the invoice it is shown as a very sophisticated computer item which has a high value. In reality, goods are coming in one container, and the value will vary based on the LC value. Inside, the goods may be old computers or some similar items. Similar is the case of various other products like silk fabric and textiles. The real value may not be to the extent of actual trade appearing in the documents given to banks.

To rub salt into the wound, these items are traded like commodity. In reality, such items are meant for specific clients, and buying high-value items requires specific market. Technological and fashion changes are very fast, and a product loses value too. With no experience in this kind of product, the banks *permitting* such trade show the appraisal approving authority's connivance.

The real activity in all the three cases was monetisation of non-funded lines of the bank and use of such mobilisation per corporates' wish and through dubious practices.

WRONG PRACTICES CASE 1-3

Use the banking lines, mostly availing non-funded lines, followed by packing loans/trust receipt/post-shipment finance for converting the facility to cash through dummy companies. Then use the funds per the investment plan. Say, out of 100 million credit lines, about 60 per cent is used for purposes other than what the facility is approved. However, a structure is created in such a way that the bank has no reason to distrust. The remaining 40 percent of funds are used for real business and also to manage due date payments. Banks allow normal operations to all the clients if the customer meets all payments on due date. This is structured trade where conduct is kept so smooth that anyone will fall prey. In the process, actual oversight is lost by the people working down the line. The misuse of bank facilities happens just under the nose of the vigilant bank staff.

These three cases have a network of their own companies as buyers who also have structured balance sheets which are used in many countries to avail financing to get additional liquidity. This liquidity keeps all the workings of the main company healthy. Cash flow management is definitely an art which these kinds of clients have created in the system to give all the controlling entities the slip. Therefore, bankers have to take extra caution in handling accounts which are too good, particularly clients using non-funded lines of closely held companies.

Real issues in sanctions done by various bank boards were permitting post-sales on an open account, while purchase leg was against the letter of credit (usance). This allowed corporates to make manipulated sales and continue to enjoy funds per their wishes. Needless to say, fund diversion/siphoning or laundering was completed much before the real problem was noticed. These cases are examples of keeping a blind eye by bank, auditors, regulators, and all concerned.

Case 4 – Hong Kong: I knew this person who was growing in the industry of mobile and other miscellaneous items during my banking time. Upon return, I found his growth to be good, and then he got India distributorship for a well-known Chinese mobile brand. In the meantime, he had also started his own mobile phone brand's assembly shop in India. All was looking good. I had helped him raise additional working capital from India through referral services.

However, ambitions ran very high, and he started diverting trading working capital to the Indian market for its own mobile manufacturing (parts still coming from China) on a bigger scale under the government incentive schemes. In banks, we are always advised to check on the diversion of funds as all Hong Kong sales started going towards the Indian arm. Banks knew but could not check in time the use of short-term working capital towards long-term uses. The manufacturing started bleeding the trading functions. Resultantly, the group made the Indian banks in Hong Kong lose heavily. The receivables in India were group companies wherein nothing would be recovered.

WRONG PRACTICES CASE 4

In a closer study of the group, when things were becoming stressful and the promoter was seeking help, I found how this group had been able to borrow substantial credit lines from Indian banks, local banks, and fund houses. In the initial period of set-up, everyone works hard to get a foothold and study the banking system. Indian banks, most of the time, are happy to lend to successful businesses who have some immovable assets also. However, the wily entrepreneur works smartly. They start with small lines with a few banks by offering 25 to 40 per cent cash collateral and make a corpus to buy immovable property, first a house and then an office. The next step is to offer this property to an existing or new bank which will provide higher credit lines. Once leveraged, cash flows are used to create more fixed assets and raise cheap financing from local banks. The irony Is that while Indian banks are offered 25 to 40 per cash collateral, local banks get 100 per cent collateral by way of mortgages. Mortgages generally are created out of bank financing and help save the company a good amount in rentals, both for business and residential, which are substantially high.

This company has also indulged in letter of credit facility monetisation where goods valuation is uncertain, but return is definitely about 97 to 98 per cent of the LC value. These funds are then used mainly to regularise bank accounts or fund more diversion to India or some other speculation. Indian banks are easy to get into this. Then they will use local companies for availing trust loans/invoice financing whereas no purchase sales are being undertaken. It is just a book entry. The helping hand gets a small amount. I have also tested this to check how the banks work. No trade documents are asked for local sales/purchase as acceptance of invoice is a good enough proof. There again, IT helps in using signatures previously obtained for any transaction.

Bankers will be worried to know how fraudulent transactions evolve. It is revealing the nature of the human brain. One product is memory card, which is costly and high in demand for various purposes. It comes in various memory capacities from very few brands like Samsung, SanDisk, etc. One small carton can be valued from US$100,000 to $300,000. This product is very volatile in prices also and can bring a fortune or big losses based on the timing of buying and selling. Therefore, real sellers and buyers prefer air shipment to save on time and avoid uncertainties of market rates.

Upon evolving, these people started getting dummy memory cards manufactured in China with identical branding or similar qualities on the packaging. These are then packed and shipped. To our unsuspecting bankers, one container of this cargo in real terms would cost more than a few million (real value not more than $15,000). These would be shipped to more lenient ports where checks and balances were less. To make things worse, for the bankers, the cargo was sold to known arms which were of no real value or use. Bankers or trade finance funds had taken insurance on the buyer. On the due date of payment, the exporter client would settle the payment through the buyer or himself if his liquidity permitted and if the purpose of funding had been served. If not, then it would be delayed as long as possible on the pretext that the buyer was not paying. Otherwise, the buyer would return the goods for quality defects and passed on the cargo to the insurers. Long story short, the loser would be the banks, by which time one of the parties would have fleeced.

Memory card/Apple product traders also work through carriers for high-value, low-volume cargo to India, thereby saving on custom duties (now GST). This is split with the team, which definitely involves our government custodians. This can be seen through immigration in how many people do frequent travel to Hong Kong, Singapore, and Dubai. Singapore will be less as they have GST. (Provision for refund is also there at the airport, provided you produce a tax paid invoice.)

Another novel method which this company used was shocking. Since our companies are debt-free and have, over the years, generated a satisfactory Dun & Bradstreet rating, most of the insurance and trade finance companies are comfortable to allow sales to our companies without us knowing how much risk can be taken on us. The most unusual part of this type of financing is that we are not aware of the insurance taken on us. Thanks to technology, the borrowing company is able to pick up our signatures from any invoice or documents issued during the course of business. These signatures are put on their invoice of sales drawn on us, and the fund house has allowed a few million against these. There is no trade transaction actually happening, nor are we aware that any invoice is issued on us. It is good till it is covered.

One fine morning, we got a liquidator notice that we had defaulted the attached invoice, and we were required to pay this sum within so many days. We were shocked to see that the event was caused by the person who took free consultations and financial help from us from time to time. We had to report the matter to police. Police are similar all over. If there is no loss, then forget it. The liquidator would start its own course. The FIR copy and a letter of reporting fraud as a good citizen were sent to us.

Case 5 – Hong Kong: This is again a reasonably old group and has substantial facilities with various banks in Hong Kong, primarily Indian banks. Local banks are almost fully secured through mortgages or some specific insurance. I will deal with insurance products separately.

As stated earlier, the balance sheets of these companies are manipulated in such a way that things look rosy all the time. Sales are increasing, profits increasing, and tax paid increasing besides payables and receivables. The parameters which normally a banker looks in the balance sheet are more or less in line with the policies of the bank. However, in reality, funds are used somewhere else, and these companies live hand to mouth. Real business is hardly 50 per cent of the balance sheet, while the remaining are entries to meet the bank requirements. If there is growth in the balance sheet, the banks will extend fresh support to take care of the mismatch in servicing of interest and overdues. At times, these companies are willing to pay a high interest for short-term mismatch to ensure that the bank accounts do not fall into NPA status. These interest rates are sometimes mind-boggling. This exercise also has been completed by me with few test cases. It became a huge task to recover the funds lent for people like us who have invested our life's savings to study the Indian promoters' behaviour or the cheating process of bank financing or other alternate lenders to the trade.

The group, well known to me since banking days, maintained a good relationship with me; and being a banker, it is always good to see a big client who can provide more information through direct interaction. With four decades of existence, one feels that the group has taken strong steps to come up to this level. But reality due to diversion of funds comes to knowledge when, every day, the client shows a stressed position. This includes the present-day situation when three to four banks have declared the company accounts NPA. The lies which these people tell are something to learn about.

All these cases which are discussed here have borrowings of over US$100 million from the system, and I am sure the tricks being played to survive on additional borrowings are the only key to their operations. Their family and kids enjoy life and study in the best locations in the world for which money is not a constraint.

This group again had opened offices in various locations around the world. It opened locally incorporated companies and, wherever possible, raised funds in these companies also. This is double financing as the goods moved from one location against Hong Kong finance are again being financed by the local lenders. Managing various location offices is a herculean task, but the principal promoters give incentive to the person managing, which helps. No one wishes to leave a paying job where he knows that if something goes wrong, then he can fly to new locations or to his home country without any liability. There are enough savings earned to help the business.

Learned many new things with this client but the surprise element was rotation of cargo. For example, company export of non-perishable cargo from China to UAE. The valuation of cargo is immaterial for this study. Once the cargo shipping documents are with the exporter, he will submit the documents to the lender for availing the finance. However, the real game is that the buyer of the cargo is party which is indirectly under the control of exporter i.e. counter party on buying side is his own entity but on paper it is shown as unrelated with the exporter. Once the cargo reaches the destination, the cargo is again rotated back to the original port of export through shipping via Malaysia and Singapore wherein exporter intermediary is added to make everything look over board and no suspicion is aroused with the lenders. At every stage intermediary keep changing but the same cargo will keep rotating for umpteen number of times. As a result there is no fresh investment on the cargo but every time finance can be availed with the bank and fund rotation keeps happening till the exporter borrower runs out of time. Really speaking one small investment of USD 10,000 to USD 25,000 helps the exporter raise finance of over 200,000 to 300,000 and funds used as per the internal plan of the promoters. Diversion through this route is very easy and difficult to catch.

Now one can understand how many clients will be doing this in the market and how many banks are being deceived. Container circulation is the safest as no one can challenge a shipment, and cargo can be valued according to choice. The liquidity thus generated is used as per promoters' needs and on due dates of export, bill payment is arranged or due date are sought to be extended. *'Keep rolling'* is the motto for small amounts, while bulk financing keeps the promoters' other interests running. Over a period, tracking the fund movement is tough, and any diversions go unnoticed. The book receivables will not yield much if the promoters so desire.

Case 6 – UAE: This group of promoters is from southern India and introduced by a common friend from the banking fraternity. I met the principal promoter and his team in Hong Kong sometime in 2016. The group is into commodities (surely doing more paperwork) and availing substantial lines through banks in UAE (maybe India too). There is no actual business, and they use our group companies as a buyer for a small fee. In my quest for finding new cases of manipulation, I have allowed companies to have a free hand so that opening up of their plan to me is easy. The operations are similar to our test case no. 3. Only the bill of lading shows the actual movement of cargo. They raise funds against such trade supplies, and then rotate the funds through layering and back to their group companies in UAE. Here, they also use insurance and funds to raise funds. I dealt with them for three years and slowly got out as time to close operations was being planned.

Case 7 – UAE/India: In fact, this party should be credited for creating interest in international commodity trading and arbitrage business therefrom while I was working in Hong Kong. He was already working for one of the leading agricultural commodity trading companies in the world. Till 2008, while working in India for the bank, we were exposed to import of commodities mainly by a few manufacturers/processors. Traders were mainly in finished steel items. We definitely had heard of a few big names like Wilmar and Glencore while handling a few cases of large Indian corporates.

However, when I landed in Hong Kong as an independent entity, he did put in his team for taking my assistance in India and UAE/Singapore, where he was having offices. This group had built up a huge turnover in no time through arbitrage trade with the help of SBI in India. It was surprising how this was going on in SBI and went unnoticed by RBI. I am sure SBI must have burnt fingers with him based on the structured merchanting trade his company was doing. The SBI trade cycle for him was completed in less than twenty-four hours after a few transactions undertaken through me wherein the LC was issued in the evening hours, and in the early morning, all documents were sent over fax. SBI issued acceptance immediately, and the letter of credit was discounted by the presenting bank and proceeds remitted per the requirement.

I am sure his Singapore/UAE entities are still helping some Indian corporates in turnover trade as well as LC monetisation through structured trade. These people know trading, with various companies being floated to give a decent look to all trading activities wherein no real business is happening, and only papers move within the banks to create a genuine trade picture to the outside world. One important thing about the promoter is that he knows how to pull the right strings with policymakers also.

Case 8 – India: This will be the crown jewel from eastern India and is already in the news. Thanks to my first contact who introduced this routing of funding to their few companies in India. Trade on papers is mainly through Russia, and all documents show rail movement in erstwhile USSR.

Initially, payments were in USD; but when some sanctions from the USA became apparent, the circulation of funds started in euro. This is still live in my company books. All deals were concluded in Singapore, and we got the papers from there and then managed payments. Thanks to past banking experience, our banking colleagues did not suspect what was going on. Though I did not have the opportunity to meet the group, I am sure this was a different kind of circulation through trade. A fair scrutiny would be possible once one got the opportunity to get into the records and the middlemen from Singapore.

HOLDING COMPANY STRUCTURES

This is another strong form of bypassing liabilities. Many Indian entities have created holding companies and subsidiary operating companies in various countries. Many times, a holding company holds only a controlling interest in subsidiaries through shares and sometimes holds some assets as, most of the time, it does not do any business. Therefore, once the subsidiary company is allowed to go bust, the least impact is on the holding company if it has not extended any commitment towards the operating subsidiary company. Again, the operating people in credit do not give much importance to the holding company mainly because it has a different location, or the promoter gives few information about it. The legal aspects of the multiple locations of a holding company and operating company are also very complex. The banks do not realise much, even if the holding company has stood as guarantor as when plans are made to run with the money, everything is done in such a way that nothing will be left for the banks. The layering is created in such a way that when you reach the bottom, there will be mud only.

It is surprising that, as a banker, we have allowed slippage from the norms during the course of operations intentionally or unintentionally. The cross-checks at various levels have also been allowed to surrender their individuality to please the head. One simple example of sanction in the merchanting trade business is that credit buying is sanctioned against an LC for 180 days, but open account sales are allowed for 180 days with no control on post-sales with the bank. The company cannot do more than two three cycles of trade but is able to show in the balance more than six cycles and then comes to the bank for additional financing. It is just simply accepted by all and sundry.

When I say this, I know that starting from branch management, concurrent auditors, internal auditors, statutory auditors, vigilance audits, and RBI inspections, all have kept their eyes closed and have enjoyed these corporates' hospitality during the course of their contractual obligations. Resultantly, a corporate is allowed to divert, siphon of, or launder money to various other points. When things totally go out of control, top management that sanctioned such lopsided facilities starts working on solutions to to temporarily defer the problem. (A borrower is allowed to buy against an LC, but sales are allowed on an open account – in reality a sales and purchase contract is already concluded when the LC is discounted overseas and proceeds brought back through advance payment.) Top management again works on supporting through evergreening and avoid the reporting of slippage as NPA or fraud during the time of the incumbent MD and CEO. Thus, he escapes any explanation or questioning.

When the matter is reported to CVC/CBI/ED, then the investigating agencies start looking at the immediate past, whereas fund movement has long been done, and only a small part is kept to keep the show running. Everything is already covered under the carpet by all. Valuable time is lost, and the trail of the money which has been out of the system becomes, at the minimum, five to seven years old. This is done through a web of companies at the disposal of the promoters.

CHAPTER 6

Other General Trading Activities Being Misused

There are various kinds of trading activities going on all across the world. My concentration is on Indian operations. I am sure people from various countries will be following to save or manipulate the regulatory system to have maximum savings. No regulatory system is found to be acceptable to people who put checks and balances as it is an individual who is running its empire. Under-invoicing and over-invoicing is common all over to save duties and also keep some funds overseas for use according to their wishes. Hawala from India is very common where goods are going through a courier.

Another route for official circulation of money is semi-precious stones. The shipments are in the region of US$200,000 to $300,000 and are shipped by air. With this, payment is sent out of India. These stones are managed to be exported again through small jewellery formation and again recycled. Real trade looks to be 20 to 30 per cent, but circulation of money is much higher from the northern Indian side. Diamond players also have a similar kind of structure, but getting into their citadel is very difficult as they are all working in a closed, veiled set-up. Various Chinese products are also being under/overvalued to save on duties in India and vice versa to keep some funds abroad. These are old and time-tested methods, but the real game is to make or save money away from the government's eyes.

IMPACT ON THE FOREX MARKET

All of the above test cases point to trading in currencies without any bona fide trade. In fact, it is akin to non-deliverable trade but only uses trade documents to move funds from one corner to another. For small gains through merchanting trade or playing with import/export activities, they wreak havoc with genuine business activities. With what we have seen during our banking days as well as from outside after getting into the shoes of these merchanting activities, I am sure they are unnecessarily inflating the country's real business data but put pressure on demand and supply for forex in the market. Our regulators and treasury handlers can guess the real impact they have on the real exchange rate for USD/INR, the major currency being used in trading activities. Let specialists in the field take up this issue.

The impact on the forex market due to these kinds of trading activities must be running into billions and affecting currency markets where such trading activities are happening on a higher scale. The artificial demand and supply for the US dollar gives an avoidable strain in the market on the local currency. I'm not an expert in the forex market, but I can say with full confidence that this has led the market into large volatility. This needs to be understood well by regulators, particularly the US Federal Reserve, which has to take note of this on priority. There are umpteen possibilities where money laundering happens in the US dollar which can be put to misuse and comes under FATF's (Financial Action Task Force) purview.

INTERNATIONAL CHAMBER OF COMMERCE (ICC)

For bankers and lending entities, the ICC issues guidelines which are very sacrosanct and treated with the right dose of drug to even out disputes in trade. This has been well tested in various courts all across the world. The major documents which the bankers/lenders use are in Uniform Customs and Practice for Documentary Credits (UCPDC) and normally related to letter-of-credit-related trading. Presently, the UCPDC

600 version is being practised. The Uniform Rules for Collections deals with the collection of trade documents.

With effect from 1 July 2007, the ICC came out with comprehensive rules by way of UCP 600 to meet the requirement of ever-changing trade practices. In this edition, for the first time, the following clause was inserted:

UCP 600 - Article 17

Original Documents and Copies
   a. **At least one original of each document stipulated in the credit must be presented.**
   b. **A bank shall treat as an original any document bearing an apparently original signature, mark, stamp, or label of the issuer of the document, unless the document itself indicates that it is not an original.**
   c. **Unless a document indicates otherwise, a bank will also accept a document as original if it:**
      i. **appears to be written, typed, perforated or stamped by the document issuer's hand; or**
      ii. **appears to be on the document issuer's original stationery; or**

     iii. states that it is original, unless the statement appears not to apply to the document presented.

    d. If a credit requires presentation of copies of documents, presentation of either originals or copies is permitted.

    e. If a credit requires presentation of multiple documents by using terms such as 'in duplicate', 'in two-fold' or 'in two copies', this will be satisfied by the presentation of at least one original and the remaining number in copies, except when the document itself indicates otherwise.

If one reads the heading, it says, 'Original Documents and Copies'. Further, under Article 17d of this article above, presentation of copy documents is permitted. Today this is the article which is being misused to its fullest which is causing great loss to trade finance lending entities all across the principal market of Asia. I am not very sure of what is happening around other parts as my access was only to Singapore, Hong Kong, and UAE. But having seen the losses to the system in the last ten years (failure of some big commodity players in Singapore and UAE), I can say for sure that this part of the article is one of the biggest reasons for defaults.

I am not sure what the reason was of the ICC think tank for inserting this clause of copy documents for LC-backed trade. However, it appears to be back-door lobbying for this clause by the large international commodity players as they are also playing with arbitrage trade on a very large scale. For me, this clause seems fine for international cargo moving by air or courier companies or for landlocked/neighbouring countries where transit time for cargo movement is very short. Presentation of copy documents in such cases is reasonable and understandable to ensure time and cost savings to the parties involved. However, long-haul marine cargo does not deserve this benefit of copy document presentation, for marine cargo (marine bill of lading, master BL, freight forwarder BL, charter party BL, etc.) is not justifiable from any angle. I would like to have a logical answer to this. I have seen and also practised to understand the implication it has for trade.

While in service at the bank in Hong Kong, one of the big international agricultural commodity representatives came with this proposal (case no. 3). He also showed some previous transaction done under the same subsection with a few banks. We were apprehensive and took time to have an internal discussion. Since this was an LC-backed trade with funding only after a swift acceptance from the LC opening bank, our internal team agreed to undertake it as the responsibility for trade was being accepted by the Bank to pay on due date. Things moved smoothly as we found that the trade was happening with full backing of cash collateral for LC issuance. In fact, the trade was only for arbitrage and book building by Indian corporates. Arbitrage was good as majority of the clients were able to build up books with transactions completed within a week. Banks had also started to accept the presentation of LC-backed documents over email/fax. This helped the smart client cash out within one to two working days and make arbitrage of 20–50 bps, depending on the deal he had been able to pull through. To sum this up, the corporates were managing banks well as each side of the trade was covered from a risk angle by the bank. No one really realised how much damage was being caused to the system on this pretext, and this is still going on.

Our Indian business people are street-smart when it comes to finding new ways to make quick money. While in service, we could not see the other side as we are blinded by the fact that we are doing a risk-free business, with full responsibility being undertaken by the LC issuing bank for honouring documents backed by copies only, and no original will be exchanged for documents. Another factor which has played its role is that arbitrage is allowed in the prime global financial markets. These kinds of products keep the treasury of big banks flowing with funds and leave a good margin. Treasury people at these banks make a good income out of huge moving funds by lending in overnight/interbank placements, a real win-win situation commercially.

Moving forward the photocopy of shipping documents gave rise to huge misuse in merchanting trade as well as in creating bogus balance sheets with corporates. High seas sales with no ownership in goods have become the order of the day. Corporates building balance sheets with a huge turnover with very little borrowing have started moving in the banks and other trade financing funds/entities for financial assistance. During this period, the corporates, particularly overseas markets where lending costs are low with banks, targeted banks for working capital. Many banks, particularly Indian PSU banks which have to work on targeted growth in top and bottom lines, have started accepting such clients with an existing client's referral. The referrals will be mainly for their connections in India or locally or for their own dummy companies.

Dummy/shell companies are mainly controlled by the person referring the client because we are doing good business with the referred company, and it will be easy for them to grow together. In reality, the funds – if approved – can be used by the referee. During the course of my stint, I developed adequate knowledge of clients using this method to deceive the banking system.

Coming back to copy transport documents being used in bank finance cases then it is more commodity items. Depending upon the need of the trader the commodity can be steel, coal, copper, iron ore, agricultural produce in bulk etc etc. Bigger traders use bulk items while smaller traders use container cargo to create trade in their books and generate receivables. The records are created with payment track records. Once few trades are created then the trader approaches insurers to Insure his trade on such entities to raise finance from his bank or trade finance units. Again, unsuspecting lenders fall prey to this trick which apparently appears to be a genuine trade. Since the balance sheets of all these entities are tailor-made to suit the lending institutions/insurers, the game of cheating begins. *It is full of accommodation trade.* Here, the high seas sales transport document for trade constitutes the starting point. While the banks ask for the original bill of lading, most of the trade finance funds do not bother about it. Many commodity players are willing to work with the trading community for arbitrage profit. Insurance brings about lack of full due diligence on the parties and trade. The following ways are adopted to help siphon of funds:

1. They are willing to lend their bill of lading for a fee, provided the entire cycle of funds is routed through them. A contract will be drawn accordingly. This ensures that there is actual trade happening. However, once the funds are released to the original shipper, then the funds are returned to the person assigning insurance policies through their other entity, thereby completing the book entries of sales and purchase. This is for book-building and fundraising. Thereafter, the responsibility to pay lies with borrower.

2. There are suppliers of bill of lading in the market – original or photocopy, depending on the need of the other party. Since banks lend against the original BL, the supplier of BL will arrange and return the original when the work is completed. In this case, consideration is charged. If the buyer of the bill of lading is not returning the BL, then the supplier makes sure that it is not misused. He can inform the master of the ship about misplacement or loss. In many cases, some shipping line employees are reported to be helping in printing extra bills of lading. Here, the sales and purchase legs are done directly by the buyer of the BL between his group companies (shown as unrelated). Insurance is taken on own entity which has the

confidence of fund raiser, and sales terms will be per insurance cover obtained. The funds so raised will be used by the principal party, and on due date, if liquidity is good and the borrowing unit wants to keep the relationship with the lending entity good, it will keep on rotating such funds till the bank exhausts its confidence. This kind of arrangement helps long-term funds for whatever purpose the borrowing entity is going to use. Thereafter, the debtor will vanish, and the insurer will be called on to pay the lender. Insurance companies are thus forced to pay the lender and allow a long-term repayment plan. If all remedies fail, then legal action and winding up are done. Smart people leave nothing or peanuts for the bank or insurance company.

3. There are a good number of funds which are active in lending against the insurance of debtors. The selling party takes insurance cover on the debtor. However, these funding parties do not bother about the shipping documents or real title over the goods. They simply look at the transport document/BL. Only a primary check whether this is actually sailing or not is taken from the International Maritime Bureau. The photocopy of the BL gives them comfort. Thereafter, it is left to the choice of the debtor when to settle. In fact, one BL copy can go to

many entities for turnover trade or help in raising finance from funds. If the parties are not able to service the debt, then it is seen that the debtor vanishes from the scene of that country. This debtor will then open a new company at a new centre, and again, the entire cycle of building books is done, the cycle of raising funds through this ingenious means.

4. Most defaulting borrowers of Indian origin have been shuffling between Singapore, UAE, and Hong Kong; and when no place is left, they will either go to India or another unknown destination. Their method of cheating with the banks has been mainly forged or manipulated in such a way that, at the end of the day, banks are left with a piece of paper only. Borrowing entities go bankrupt, while the promoter enjoys another destination with the money.

5. Insurance entities are struggling day in and day out to cover the lenders and are now slowly leaving the commodity market. The amount of dirt they have gathered over the last few years is mainly due to the shipping documents – copy documents where there is no genuine trade but a game to raise finance. There is no intention to pay but to leave the place once the lender also raises his hands. The borrower will look for a new well to quench his appetite.

6. Besides various players who are not into commodities but in general trading, the invoice plays a much bigger role besides the shipping document. Here, two types of shipments are done. It can be a full container load (FCL) or less container load (LCL). The valuation of goods can vary from one to fifty times of the real value. It is difficult to verify in the container that the shipment has taken place. Various goods have different qualities and rates. C-rated goods can be summed up as of A+ quality and valued. There is a complete possibility of dummy goods also inside the container.

7. I feel bad that I could not reach the original source of the bill of lading suppliers in the market who help clients raise funds from the banking system. Only intermediaries have approached and provided the required support to willing parties through me. However, with three to four years on this trade aspect, I am sure that some shipping agents and people having access to internal documents at big commodity players are able to make some quick money from the market. Merchanting trade of Indian corporates is the result of this effort.

Every day is a learning experience in the international trade. The bigger the player, the bigger are the chances of manipulating the system. There will be a good number of examples available from the Singapore/UAE market where circulation of money through trade transaction is happening with Indian clients. Hong Kong is much below these countries, thanks to Chinese control. Commodity leads the way. Many trade finance funds are facing the real music in funding such trade backed by insurance. Few funds may be filing for bankruptcy too per feedback available from the market.

A study of some of the big trading names which failed recently in Singapore/UAE who were dealing in commodities causing big defaults in banking system were dealing in bulk commodities. However, majority of Indian entities which were dealing in commodities the amount of default would be less and commodity used by these traders are frequently traded items like copper, steel or similar small cargos. This kind of trade does not attract more scrutiny. Some of the big defaulters of Indian banks are available with the respective banks in Hong Kong, Singapore, and UAE. A study of the reason for default will make one understand what is being done by our own people in the name of trade. I have restricted my reading on these people only. I have done a live experiment with some of these people only.

These very people thereafter ask the bank to settle for ten to twenty cents over a period so that they can restart from these very places by building up balance sheets again. Our database and memories are short. We are ready to listen to the stories on learning from past experience from these very people and fall prey again.

The International Maritime Bureau has done studies and has also made observations on the reality of the trade bill of lading, and per my sources, there is no clarity about what action is being taken by regulatory agencies. Seems it again lies as a low priority item on their list. Continuous suffering by lenders will continue if real steps are not taken forthwith. Time has come to find real action on this front.

In a nutshell, Bill of Lading has become a product for trading and is being used like a leased or use-and-pay item.

CHAPTER 7

The Protectors

The PSU financial sector's misdemeanours are controlled by various arms decided by the policies approved by the government of India. The primary arm is internal control through the CVO deputed by the GOI. Once the matter goes out of control, then the role of the chief vigilance commissioner, CBI (anti-corruption bureau), and enforcement directorate comes into the picture.

Financial mischief is done with connivance from within, from within with help from an outsider, and totally from outside. I will not deal with small mischief done by small thieves from within. They cause more reputation damage than financial damage and demoralise the people working in the field. However, bigger mischief is done from within with the connivance of the people at the top, mainly large credit matters. Many times, one party who is lower in hierarchy will succumb to the pressure of the people at the top and sign on dotted lines. These people are not fully aware of what has been the understanding between the top management and the corporate. Here, the top management also ensures that it has to take care of the members on the board as credit decisions are approved by the management committee of the board. One point which is very important is that the management committee in PSU banks has to have one CA director in all meetings besides permanent members of MD/EDs. The CA director is appointed by GOI, and he along with the team of these people wreaks havoc with personal agenda as well as his political bosses/bureaucrats who help in its furtherance. Very rarely will one find clean people from this group on the bank's board per my experience.

In good old times of, say, fifteen to twenty years back, government/RBI nominee directors were also part of the management committee; but subsequently, they eased out to avoid scrutiny. The government nominee director is mainly from the financial services department with the rank of joint secretary. Needless to say, His Master's Voice prevailed in free play to the team formed by the political bosses. Financial sanctions/disbursement of loans from 2002 onwards will stand as testimony to this fact. This has been echoed in the parliament also by the present-day government.

Big loans attract good effort, and many times, all forces are applied to get the loan application moving fast. It is not an easy task for a large amount to be considered without going through the rigmarole of processes. It may be a little less cumbersome for an existing client but is more rigorous for new projects. In PSU banks, majority of the time, a big-value new business starts from the top to the bottom, whereas it has to be from the branch upwards. This practice has become prevalent since the late 1990s onwards.

In such cases, everyone in the process is from within. In case a default happens, the first line of defence is to protect everyone in the chain. However, if some head has to roll, then the person below who has processed is put to maximum discomfort. The poor guy does not know how to manage things as everyone puts the blame squarely on him; that was why he did not bring this to notice while working as dictated from above. The internal control of the top management plays a vital role so that the matter is not sent to the CVC. Even the CVO coming from different banks tows the line of the top management. There will be a huge number of examples to throw light on this aspect.

When decisions are taken at the board level, then the system does not demand accountability on the people making such high-value decisions. It Is observed that such meetings are over within a short time and without deliberations. It is called management of board members as all are coming through the channel of the government, and it is hard to create issues at this level. 'Keep everyone happy' is the motto.

THREE ARMS (INDIAN CONTEXT)

The government exercises control on the financial sector through various regulators, and in India, it is RBI, CVC, and their extended arms CBI/ACB and ED mainly. The Central Vigilance Commission is headed by a constitutional authority (i.e. a chief vigilance commissioner and two vigilance commissioners - VC), while the CVC is an IAS cadre officer (mainly retired), one VC from IPS and one retired banker (chairman/ MD). All these positions come only after good lobbying by the occupant of the position. From whatever I have observed in my career, I am convinced that these people are there to protect their respective cadres; and if their political bosses fall in the trap, then all these agencies will jointly come to protect them through whatever manipulations possible, though RBI/CVC might have a less important role to play than CBI/ED in matters against the political bosses.

There seems to be an unwritten commandment as we hardly see any serious action against the people who hold the position of ED/MD in the financial sector. If the person is sitting as vigilance commissioner and others have senior positions, then they will know how large corporate exposure works at all PSU banks. Nothing moves without the go signal from the top. (Actually, majority of matters involving large exposures start at the top – be it through corporates directly or through the masters of the political scenario.) Just ask privately some of the people suffering at the senior level, and they will confirm that they have followed instructions and are now facing the music.

The highly learned people at the top in the bank make mistakes knowingly to please or appease and, in the process, also make their future safe. A scrutiny of big corporate failures will expose the games, but the question is, when the powers that be work towards saving the skin of those who worked with ulterior motives, how can justice be heard? It is well known in the market that the top authority in any bank plays the game for money, but nothing is done to prevent it. How much lobbying is done to get to that position, and the choicest bank is well known to everyone at the bank.

If someone gets into the net, then things will be made so slow that things will die its natural death. I have seen actions initiated ten years back that are still stuck as a pipe dream. The guilty may be having some headache due to this, but it is made sure that things do not come to the final stage. These very people then throw back the ball in the court of the people who have processed it.

In Indian Police system corruption rules, higher officers continue to be in news for wrong reasons but this news is allowed to die and nothing serious is done to pursue the corruption angle. It is felt that the loyalty of these officers lies with the corporate fraudster rather than with the government who is accountable to the common man whose money has been swindled through the banking system. Again, all systems have exceptions and good people are also there but are usually outnumbered. IAS is working with his political boss all the time, so he knows where the power comes from and which side he has to work. If not cooperating, he will be shifted to nondescript functions.

All the three combined have to also look for culpability of political masters. When the political master is in trouble, then all three work to see that such efforts to make him accountable are thwarted with full force. 'Save the master' is the motto now. There is no need to elaborate this point, which all now see openly, but they are the law now.

I had to deal with CBI investigating officers on a few occasions during the course of my employment with the bank in Mumbai as well as outside the bank. I feel sorry for these people who have to be spoon-fed for their job, yet they find that the bank has erred. The Investigating Officer (IO) is primarily a policeman and is not aware of financial matters, unlike the expert fraudster or the corporates who have a team full of financial experts at their disposal. The IO, being not up to the mark, tries to use the language of a policeman on the street, which does not help the cause of any investigation. Any investigation requires homework through the records taken in possession, and only pointed questions need to be asked related to the case. It is a known fact that these investigating officers are more inclined to favour corporates as they are able to make things easy for them. To work on any case, they try to squeeze in whatever kinds of financial gains they can take from the banks too. The bank officer at the lower level is framed for deviation and penalised. In operational banking, many times, oral instructions prevail or are dictated. This is why banking legally is known as Practice & law of Banking where many times, practice has to prevail as decisions are taken based on logic and circumstances. Various decisions are well accepted in Practice and have been accepted in the courts too.

Looking at other similar kinds of agencies, the standard of investigation is almost the same or slightly better at the senior level also. All think of applying pressure on the people called during the course of investigation. Harassment of people is preferred to extract information. The statements are recorded under duress, and the language which the accused or witness tries to give is not accepted, but the language of the IO prevails. The IO knows that the statement can be easily retracted in the court as he has not been allowed to get his own version recorded. The hard nuts are always difficult to break, and it requires some smart thinking to get to the bottom of the case. All boxes need to be ticked properly before putting any investigation report before the legal system. Majority of the time, the IOs cut a sorry figure in the courts.

Investigating officers in investigation point to certain procedural lapses without having procedural knowledge of the subject. How they arrive at these lapses is not known but become expert on these matters by just throwing the ball in the court. There are instances where the person responsible for wrong decision is not taken to account or the person who was responsible for monitoring these are allowed to go scot free. In majority of the big loans board level people are responsible for procedural lapses but there it is treated as decision by committee. The real culprits in such cases are vested interest of Top Management people.

There is no natural justice. Investigating officers' actions become bone in the neck of the alleged accused. The wrongs done by them makes it a life sentence for the honest officers who get penalised. The penalties result in life long depression and avoidance of sitting on the decision process. Thereafter, these people get labelled as negative people. Good number of officers remain aloof and always curse the superiors who made their life sentence so painful mentally.

Then again, multiple agencies work on similar omission and commission of frauds, leading to wastage of manpower. It will be in order if a combined team is formed, or if one party feels that the case has another angle, then that specialised team will be required do the job, but the judicial course of action must be at one place. In financial matters time lost is money lost. Be it at Bank level or at the level of investigating agencies who take their own time in helping the culprits play with the evidence on record.

All the three arms know what is being done by the head of the particular institution but no evaluation is done on the legacy left by them. The moment head of financial institution leaves, the financial health becomes visible and so do the acts of omission and commission done by him and his team.

CHAPTER 8

Legal System

Having seen the legal system in India and a few countries, I find that our Indian legal system lacks the punch. In financial cases, if there is adequate ground for prosecution, a summary trial is required. However, the cases drag for years. I know of a case which I initiated in 1986 but was not concluded till 2001. (My witness was called in this year.) All documentary evidence was against the accused. When we see such cases getting decided in a few months overseas like Hong Kong, Singapore, and UAE, then it definitely gives a clear indication that our system needs a big overhaul. Professionalism is missing from our legal system. Delay is the order of the day. During our banking times, we have seen so many cases where our legal system has let the financial system down in straightforward cases, and they get into non-relevant issues.

All special courts established are again doing the same process of delayed justice. The judges should have a cell which should examine the petitions as a lot of government cases lack a real professional approach. The motive of the department is to get rid of the matter once they reach a dead end. Motive of the investigating arms is that let the onus be on the defendant all the time. This is justice denied as half baked inputs will not result in to a good result. In the present-day market all across the world, there are a good number of competent people who will be able to understand complicated matters from the financial world and take or suggest correct steps to stop the malice. Further, many times, scrutiny of the filing by the government agencies is not at all done, but all who are found in channel are made prima facie accused; and many times, people are sent to jail without being heard. Then these people waste time and money to procure bail and then contest the case. By putting the people in jail at the initial stage and without being heard, it makes justice a farce. The legal system should speak for its value and must come out of futile efforts for genuine justice. Lack of competence should not rule the legal system.

The real role the legal system can play is to get hold of Indian people who cheat the banking system overseas and then sit in cosy corners in India or some other country where holding the person is not difficult, but again, the question is, who will bell the cat? I see Indian courts issuing summonses to Indians overseas or foreign passport holders to appear in Indian court. However, the same system is not taking any action against Indians who have cheated the Indian banks in other countries and sitting pretty in Indian homes, taking shelter under the legal umbrella of jurisdiction. People have given personal guarantees too which can be enforced. But again, the judicial system is blind in taking initiative, suiting the people who have laundered money. It is a hard fact. The system which has the authority to give clear direction to the executive fails miserably on this count.

Why is our legal system not taking the support of technology and ordering brain mapping or narco tests on the promoters of corporates who have cheated huge amounts from the system? Today technology and artificial intelligence can help a lot in getting to the bottom of many crimes. Once the legal system works towards this, there is an extreme possibility that programme writers will be able to come up with a very strong software support to nail the culprits in time and save valuable time. So far, delays have helped clients dispose of assets in such a manner that finding the trail becomes very tough.

All these protectors have not brought out any solid recovery to the banks and might have caused more loss due to delayed decisions on various pretexts. These trends are common and unique to our control structure. The bank's top management is shirking responsibility, and all major defaults are being reported as credit frauds. This way, if any harm comes to the top management of yesteryears, then no one can put a finger on the person making a report. However, nothing concrete happens as investigations take long years, and longer years get used in courts.

The first thing which our legal system should do is to entrust the high-value financial crimes to courts headed by retired justices who can understand their nuances faster than our small and lower courts who are saddled with large number of cases. Their system is not ready to understand complexities, nor do they have adequate exposure to complex accounting frauds which are structured in such a way that will look like flawless work to a common man. Judiciary at lower levels has often been compromised to favour the big and influential. Bankers at grassroots level have also not been able to make heads or tails of such transactions.

REGULATORY ROLES

For Indian banks, the RBI is the supervisor of all financial activities. Similarly, all countries have their regulators. RBI supervision is mainly with a practising banker who is inducted from commercial banks after completing tenure as MD/CEO. If one has met the supervisory authorities of a few countries, then a comparison is definitely made. The supervision is done on-site as well as off-site by the regulatory authorities. They go to branches as well as the controlling office. However, I find that there is a vast difference in supervision from the RBI. Our regulators only believe in shooting out guidelines. There is no real follow-up and seeing the culmination of instructions to a logical level. In Singapore and Hong Kong, one relationship officer is continuously monitoring and also calling for one-to-one discussion to put things to end, duly complying.

However, on fraud follow-up, there is definitely no clarity. It becomes a data entry for every regulator. Follow-up may be by way of an advisory that such fraudulent event has happened and for the banks to take precaution. No individual bank also does any follow-up, whereas this can be done through audit arms. Audit arms have really failed, even though internal audit is conducted by their own officers as well as trained/

semi-trained outside agencies. The real reason is lack of follow-up action.

I also warned the RBI/CVC (see last pages as exhibits) twice on merchanting trade, but no action seems to have been taken; otherwise, an alarm bell must have become active. I also know that anonymous letters are thrown into the dustbin and that giving one's name makes the life of the complainant more difficult with agencies and brings threats of various kinds. I am sure something will happen now.

One incident needs to be quoted here. While working in Hong Kong, we came across a fraudulent BL from our client. The client was into metal trading and was a Singapore Permanent Resident/passport holder. He was recognized as top SME client for the last two years (2009-10) and given due publicity through Print Media. We immediately took action by filing an First Information Report and also made our report to HKMA/HO/RBI per procedures. We went one step ahead by filing our complaint with the Monetary Authority of Singapore (MAS). We definitely expected some quick action against a fraudulent action of their citizen. However, to our surprise, they felt offended by our reporting to them. In our view, it would have initiated quick action to pass on the information to the right wings of their financial crime investigating authority for arriving at a logical end. It means countries will handle cases that happened on their soil only. The ultimate result was that the person vanished to unknown destination with good number of banks from Singapore/Hong Kong/Malaysia suffered financially.

Further, the money laundering aspect is the responsibility of regulators as they come across all the events happening through the banking or hawala channel. However, the efforts in this direction suggest that we are beating around the bush as regulatory efforts start so late that the trail is lost. Even if the enforcement directorate is able to get hold of such assets with conclusive evidence, they will sit on them for so long that the real impact is lost, and legal battles further complicate matters.

Based on experience gained over the years and the procedures being followed at various banks, it is certain that top corporates are able to make the branch people their puppets and get away with a large number of procedural bottlenecks. They are also able to manage the local auditors (including concurrent auditors). If someone tries to make noise, then the concerned officer gets the flak. No need to explain this in detail.

It is time for the RBI to let merchanting trade become history and introduce further restrictions. The world has moved on and is very closely linked under the WTO network. Countries are working closely on very specific trade deals. We cannot go on with outdated models of trade just to please certain traders. Tax benefits for exports are good if one is a net foreign exchange earner.

During the course of assessment, I can say with certainty that the Indians' favourite joint for money laundering is the triangle of Singapore, UAE, and Hong Kong. Hong Kong is the last mainly due to reasons best known to the people involved. In the Indian system, one tends to believe that money can buy anything, and reports of culprits can be tweaked in such a way that the accused finds a way out, while many times the one who has done the hard work with good intention is penalised or put to such misery that the initiated action becomes irrelevant and dies in time.

Further, starting from the top management of the banks to the level of all protectors, it can be said that the manipulative and scheming people are called farsighted visionaries as they temporarily make things look rosy; but in a short time after their departure, the real picture emerges. Again, with the cover-up operations, people tend to forget as too many things are happening all across the country.

CHAPTER 9

Summing Up

All of the above and many small things have been done by me to understand things from within. I am sure majority of the things will be in the knowledge of our accounting people in the industry, but for beginners, a lot of things will become clear. These types of trade should come under accounting fraud. Helping industrial finance and a real project is good, but the trading activity has to be done against proper security/checks and balances. There is no need to go overboard in supporting trade. Trade comes with a quick turnaround of cash or equivalent. It is to be seen whether trade is handled with thorough professionalism. Credit terms in trade are very short, and cash can exchange hands, but book entries will continue indefinitely. Thereafter, these will continue to be available as current assets/ dead assets; and ultimately, the finance extended will become non-realisable. In the international trade, it is observed that majority of trade finance comes with a lot of tighter norms and securities.

Our Indian banks will have to reconsider strategy and forget what we are taught in India. To evolve locally is the real challenge. The test cases given have used the system only to siphon of funds on the post-sales leg, where nothing was done at all levels in the sanctioning and disbursement processes. Needless to say, operational people were kept under pressure for helping rather than going for serious compliance. The internal control points through various audits have also sidestepped their own guidelines. This applies to the regulator level too.

I have a feeling that our investigating agencies must have proper full training. Financial and white-collar crimes are done by people who are way ahead of people who are assigned the task of finding the truth. It is also felt that investigating agencies will rope in the right kind of mix in their teams which can help reach the destination faster rather than things dragging for many, many years, by which time all trace and interest is lost. Remaining time is lost in long-drawn legal battles. The money is lost, and the person has to account for it legitimately. I hope the real work will continue to make things better for the banking and financial world.

My suggestion to the regulatory and legal authorities in all these places will be to go for quick action and not just sit over things. Indians, in particular, have created a huge web of companies in different structures just for the sake of bookkeeping, while the real cash moves with the kingpin. Accounting norms for maintaining records is also limited, and once the goal is achieved, the people and records will vanish in thin air. Take actions which create fear in the minds of culprits. The legal system is being used by these players, and experts are defending these very people who have ill-gotten money.

I'll end with some suggestions for the regulatory and financial crime checking authorities with the hope that some aspects of this study will help the bankers and insurers who are already poorer by billions of dollars because of mischievous customers. The people in authority have to work on corroborating things and find where the system has gone wrong which has led the cancer of corruption and fraudulent practices to go uncontrolled. May wiser sense prevail among the people who matter to bring a healthy system for the financial sector's survival.

Action Points Suggested

a. Third-party bill of lading must not be taken while extending bank finance. There are provisions in the shipping system where a new master bill of lading can be issued in lieu of the surrender of an existing master bill of lading. This will create proper records. Some system can be created to get the trail of bills of lading issued. 'To order' Bill of Lading to be avoided and BL with consignee name appearing or ultimate goods receiver to appear as Notify party.

b. Freight forwarder bill of lading must not be accepted for financing. In this case, the master bill of lading holds control of the cargo till the end, and only the MBL holder can ask the shipping line to release. This practice is there to ensure that payment is received by the shipper. There will be a good number of cases where people or the financier have gotten stuck in this process.

c. All financial defaults of over US$5 million relating to lending to trade must be put to rigorous scrutiny by investigating agencies/regulators in India/Singapore/UAE/Hong Kong. In any trade, full loss is not possible unless the cargo has been obtained fraudulently from exporter. All traders make best use of their efforts to salvage the situation even at a deep discount or haircut. Real investigation will throw light on how much has been diverted / laundered.

d. Where borrowers have left the country after committing default, it must be seen as financial crime, and their names must be given to Interpol to ensure their movement is checked by other countries. This is a very big grey area where these defaulters move with the funds to new centres to establish business and then create a new default scenario.

e. Trade finance funds must have similar due diligence on bill of lading, and parties must check misuse of funds generated through trade. Many times, these funding entities have the backing of insurance companies which extend protection to sellers. However, insurers pay for slack supervision by these fund houses as, a large number of times, trades are given legitimate camouflage which cannot be ascertained without clear understanding.

f. The investigating arms of various government agencies all across the world need to know the full trade cycle processes to assess the cases referred to them.

g. Majority of financial defaults will come under the money laundering category. A minimum benchmark must be set up by regulators, and thereafter, the legal system must take up these cases on the fast track. The directors of such defaulting companies must be quarantined during this period so that they are not able to influence and compromise evidence.

h. Shipping lines have to start working on the block chain technology. We have been hearing about this, but there seems less progress on this.

i. The integrity of the system has to improve to bring higher professionalism. Indians have failed at many fronts which were the subject of this study. It is clear, however, that bad practices are prevailing in many territories. Singapore and UAE will be the best examples of such events where many nationalities work with big numbers and vanish.

j. Only permanent residents must be considered for credit facilities with lots of caution. Follow local practices rather than the parent bank's practices.

k. If any proposal is originating from sources within the bank, then it should be properly recorded.

EPILOGUE

I dedicate this study to my honest banking colleagues who have suffered in their personal banking careers wherein they had to bow to the pressure of their superiors, particularly people at the very top. I owe an apology to the people who accidently suffered during my tenure as their superior, but these were the people who motivated me to set foot in this field to understand the games played behind the bankers' back. It is time for such people to come out and speak the truth instead of silently suffering mentally. There are a good number of officers who have become party to unwanted decisions just because they were sitting on the seat at the wrong time. I know a good number of people who just could not push back the efforts of their superiors without avoiding backlash or suffering harsh humiliation. I hope this study helps curtail some of the bad practices of the corporate clients and also make officers aware of the pit falls in handling export import documents or local documents under Letter of Credits or trade finance. More logical and analytical scrutiny of documents would improve the knowledge that will become part of the job on routine basis.

This study may ruffle some feathers and may be the tip of an iceberg but the fact remains that there is need for serious working on holding the mighty ones accountable on priority. Compromises being made would not bring the change.

Truth must prevail. Dishonest not to sit on judging the honest. First and the next step in the right direction is need of the hour.

ABBREVIATIONS USED

1. SEEUY   – Self Employment Scheme for Educated Unemployed Youth
2. SEPUP   – Self Employment Programme for Urban Poor
3. DRI   – Differential Rate of Interest Scheme of lending
4. IRDP   – Integrated Rural Development Programme
5. SC/ST   – Scheduled Caste & Scheduled Tribe
6. IAS   – Indian Administrative Service
7. CVC   – Chief Vigilance Commission/ Commissioner
8. CBI   – Central Bureau of Investigation
9. ED   – Enforcement Directorate
10. FS   – Finance Secretary (Secretary Financial Services)
11. M.Com   – Management Committee of Board
12. PSU   – Public Sector Undertaking of Govt
13. RR   – Railway Receipt
14. BL   – Bill of Lading
15. FIR   – First Information Report

16. SPV	–	Special Purpose Vehicle
17. AML	–	Anti-Money Laundering
18. RBI	–	Reserve Bank of India
19. FEMA	–	Foreign Exchange Management Act
20. CMD	–	Chairman & Managing Director
21. AGM/ DGM/GM	–	Assistant/Deputy/General manager
22. CA	–	Chartered Accountant
23. NPA	–	Non Performing Asset
24. SBI	–	State Bank of India
25. HO	–	Head Office
26. SFIO	–	Serious Fraud Investigation Office
27. ZM	–	Zonal Manager
28. LC	–	Letter of Credit
29. BL	–	Bill of Lading
30. AWB	–	Airway Bill
31. DA	–	Documents against Acceptance
32. BPLR	–	Benchmark Prime Lending Rate
33. BPS	–	Basis Points
34. HNI	–	High Net worth Individuals

Mr.Arun Jaitley,
Finance Minister,
Govt of India,
A-44, Kailash Colony,
New Delhi – 110048.

Dear Mr.Jaitley,

I was part of Indian Banking System for over three and a half decades and have seen things from very Close angle. I always made efforts and followed certain strict parameters on character degeneration but was not in a position to stop people going overboard in doing wrong things at the top level. Down the line things were and are more or less cleaner vis a vis Top Management. The top Management including the Board of Directors (sold by Govt of India representatives at a cost), govt directors, Ministry of finance officials and to top it all the central ministers at Delhi were literally screwing the system through their bunnies. The sufferers were the officers in the middle and senior management ranks who were exposed to CBI/CVC. These officers were and are not in a position to say a word against the top management knowing fully well that if they utter any leading point towards them then they are going to be doomed forever as system is more towards the top people and clients who bribe the CBI officials and ensure that no one points a finger at them. CBI officials would never go into the details of who brought the default borrower company closer to the bank leading to huge losses to the Bank but would only place blame on the officers at the ground level through the post mortem process. Employee directors are more or less sold out to the top management for peanuts thrown by the Management.

I am working on an eye opener for the public through my network now and would show to the world and Indian public the rape of banking system by high and mighty. I am giving myself 2 years to complete my investigation and gather all the evidences by involving myself with the shady network of consultants and brokers and directors appointed by the Govt of India. I will tear apart the chameleons in the system and will expose people who ripped apart the system at the cost of honest people working in the banking system. The honest people are not allowed to go up the ladder beyond a point or if someone reaches a good level he is assigned tasks which do not do justice to their caliber and skills.

Be ready for the blow. In a few months from now I shall start sending you the chains of disclosures which would have wide ramifications for the Indian banking system once things start falling apart. I know this is a herculean task but the right people would come forward once the issue is raised through proper media. I will also disclose my identity at the right time.

Get ready for the real assault. I am not going to leave the system into the hands of politicians, bureaucrats, consultants, top management and other brokers/business men syndicates. I am with right kind of people who mean good for the system and the country. The sufferers' voice needs to be raised at the right level. Someone has to bell the cat and I have taken up this task.

Victim & Crusader

The Governor,
Reserve Bank of India,
Central Office, 16th Floor,
Shaheed Bhagat Singh Marg,
Mumbai 400 001.

Chief Vigilance Commissioner,
Central Vigilance Commission,
8, Satarkata Bhavan, INA Road
INA Colony, New Delhi 110023.

Mr.Raghuram Rajan,
Governor,
Reserve Bank of India,
Central Office,
Mumbai 400 021.

Dear Sir,

Bogus Trade routes/circular trade in
Domestic and international market by
Indian corporates

I had written one letter in Mid November 2014 which was addressed to FM, CVC, Governor RBI and one advocate fighting against corrupt practices mainly against Govt. I had also informed that I am also a retired senior executive of a big nationalized Bank and have seen things from close angle at all levels in the Bank including Board/M.Com where decisions are taken.

I had advised that I am now investigating big games played by these corporates by becoming a part of the process which is helping me know lot of things including modus operandi of corporates working towards their own goal by beating the system at its own game and make huge profits without investing any serious money of their own. The Banks, including SBI, are part of guinea pig for these corporates who have been able to give a sugary pill to all at the top.

I am very close to collecting evidences at both the fronts. However, as I would prefer to be a Ghost all the time (cannot afford to risk my life if I come in open) as I am getting all the information by working with them and would not like any doubts about my role. It may happen that I May decide to come in open at an appropriate time but before that I would like that RBI to strengthen Systems wherein fraudsters' to be grilled under lie detector tests and identity of the whistle blower is kept intact all the time. The amounts involved run into billions and may have big impact on the reputation of the country and banking system. Hence, a proper evidence needs to be collected to make sure cleaning operations do not get lost in official system of our country.

As already told that I am a crusader now to get things changed for good for ever. People like me have paid the price of misadventures of politicians, top management and board level people besides bureaucrats sitting in the Finance ministry at Delhi or at some important places including our watchdog at CVC. Their names would also be brought out with substantial role model they play in the decision process of vested interests.

I can make use of other sources of disclosures but I am looking at the broader picture of correction instead putting the country and banking systems reputation at high risk. In my next communication I will give you certain suggestions with reasoning which can be put in place suddenly to give shock to these corporates and thereafter you will be able to identify why and how the trade to defraud the system is done.

Trust Me on facts

Copy to:

The Finance Minister,
Govt of India, New Delhi.

Mr.Raghuram Rajan,
Governor,
Reserve Bank of India,
Central Office,
Mumbai 400 021.

Dear Sir,

Bogus Trade routes/circular trade in Domestic and international market by Indian corporates

I have been writing to you few times since last one and half year.

Now I think I have done enough work to expose businesses harming in forex market to the Banks. However, how do I trust the system which sucks us. It will not save the right person and nothing will happen unless whistle blowers identity & life is properly protected. In fact main issue is that the system should work on the correct information provided rather than find the person who has provided information and in the meantime allow the culprits keep swindling the system.

So, please come up with proper guidelines. Will pass on information which would Have far reaching implications on the banking and forex market. Just get hold of the corporates without much publicity otherwise banking system will have serious problems. The problems are legacy driven but will become feeder for bad publicity as majority of the bankers are innocent and working totally in good faith.

Now, I look forward to some proper steps safety of people sharing the information and keeping the identity too deeply covered like RBI is not ready to expose defaulters. We must be kept away from the glare to defend our action rather it is the system which has to act to get hold of wrong doers.

I will keep watching the actions but would pass on some concrete information soon.

Trust me on facts

Dear Shri █████   *emailed*

Risk management –
Diversion of funds through front firms/companies
<u>By Real estate dealers/importers</u>

It is more than 6 months that I am at the helm of New Delhi Zone which has a high incidence of NPA as well as stressed accounts. Every month we have been struggling to save the accounts from slipping to NPA status through recovery of critical amount but no real recovery is seen in the normal course of business. On a scrutiny of various accounts I am of the firm opinion that people in real estate business/import business are trying to deceive the Banking system through innovative means as they are trying to build up real estate inventories for future profits.

In the real estate sector as the credit exposure is not easily available from Banks, the builders/small time property dealers are forming trading/import export companies and take non-funded LC limits with usance of 180 days or funded export credit limits (EPC/FBP). The facilities are covered with collateral of immovable property/ies. The LC or EPC is taken in favour of either group companies or their associates in the business (not declared at the time of proposal). There is no real trade transaction but documents are presented under the LC to the opening Bank which is accepted by the borrower company for payment on due date. Upon acceptance getting conveyed to the document handling Bank, the same is negotiated at the lowest possible rate and the funds used to buy properties (mostly stressed properties). Similar route is adopted for taking EPC & then converting them into FBP (a cycle goes for one year almost). In the process the borrower/associates get white money at low cost. Thereafter, payment of LC on due date is almost not there and devolvement is cleared with lot of difficulty as the property is not sold at targeted price besides part of the money is received in cash (unaccounted black money). Export bills also do not get realized in time. Resultantly, the accounts continue to be under stress. Bank is thus put in vicious cycle to support such accounts and they will continue to offer additional securities for servicing overdues and/or take fresh LC to support their business of property dealing. In the process devolvement and interest servicing is getting serviced by additional financing against additional security of properties. The borrowers continue to enjoy low cost funds for speculative activities. It is almost impossible to get out of these accounts unless a decision to exit the account is taken by stopping support & making the account NPA or converting the working capital lines into Demand/Term Loans payable over a period of 2-3 years. Exit would be at a loss or max at book outstanding.

Second dimension to the above process is that the borrowers non funded LC facilities and raise money against discounting of LCs in associate companies from other Banks, say at overall cost of 12% p.a. and lend in the market at 2-3% thereby making a clean income of 1.5 to 2% at our cost. Bank is feeling safe that it has taken fully secured non fund exposure with collaterals of less than facilities or full value. Borrower also enjoys

130

concessions as it has leveraged its immovable properties. Bank is also stuck when LC payment is due & devolvement is order of the day. These are high risk accounts.

Another dimension, which the builders are doing in the above game, is that builders are floating building material firms/company and take funded/non funded limits. While the funded lines against building material items help them raise cash at SME rates but in fact the funds are used by them for acquiring land banks or holding on the inventory of unsold/under construction flats to jack up the flat prices. Non funded lines are apparently used to raise finance but the trade deals appear to be questionable.

Overall there apparently is circumvention of system to go for real estate business under camouflage of trade. This may be happening in other centres also particularly in metros. We can break this trend if we are willing to take temporary hits in our asset portfolio or converting the exposure to real estate but would make things quite transparent. It also appears that similar trend is being used in imports where devolvement of LC happens for good and accounts become NPA. It is again possible that goods are sold in the market while Bank is committed to make payment of import LCs but no payment would come from company on due dates. There are some DRI cases in respect of import/exports where transactions are purported to be dubious in nature. Export fronts by property dealers are also helping them take low cost export funds, duty draw back etc and payments are normally settled through questionable routes (exports are actually not there or some insignificant items are exported in connivance). This is a systematic plan to overcome rules/regulations in the Banking system particularly in real estate sector. I am afraid Bankers are playing into the hands of smart borrowers and are inviting trouble for functionaries at field level who would be unknowingly exposing themselves to SAR from vigilance angle as colluder with the customers.

This aspects needs to be discussed at appropriate level to control assets portfolio from getting sticky through diversion of funds.

With regards,

131

www.ingramcontent.com/pod-product-compliance
Lightning Source LLC
Chambersburg PA
CBHW032026170526
45157CB00002B/862